Blood Ties
Language in the Blood
Book 2
By Angela Lockwood

First published on Amazon KDP (ebook) January 2015

Amazon Createspace (print) September 2015

ISBN-13: 978-2955405307 (Angela Lockwood)

ISBN-10: 2955405302

To my husband Adam, my editor Penny and the SNCF, without them this book would certainly have come off the rails somewhere and not reached its final destination.

Contents

Contents

Chapter 1: Jean-Claude

It was in early spring 2013 that I got into a black sedan with Jean-Claude Bernard of the DCRI, the French secret police. As I took my seat next to him, I'd already started doubting that turning myself in to get my friend George Baxter released from prison was such a good idea. I knew it was the right thing to do, though. I *had* killed a woman and it had had nothing to do with George, but I was a vampire – doing the right thing wasn't really my style.

George and I had been friends since about 1986 owing to a promise I'd made to his grandfather. I'd felt guilty for turning George senior into a vampire during World War Two and had been keeping an eye on his family since the 1950s. They hadn't needed my help until young George had threatened to go off the rails. He was older and wiser now and *most* of the time he now kept me in check. He had a grown-up daughter, Emily and it was she who had sought my help when her father was arrested for murder. George and Emmy were amongst the few people who knew my real nature, but that was about to change. The French secret service agents were about to get the fright of their lives.

Jean-Claude Bernard was taking me to the DCRI headquarters north of Paris at Levallois-Perret. He looked to be in his mid-fifties, with thinning black hair that had started to go grey at the temples. He was dressed in a sensible, dark grey, polyester suit that looked like it had been bought about ten years ago and worn to work most days since. It had become rather tight, a fact I imagined was due to some fine French cuisine and an obviously sedentary lifestyle. He'd probably been an agent for many years and all original thought and humour had long since departed.

I'd taken an immediate dislike to the guy, an opinion justified by the static shock I got off his cheap and nasty synthetic suit when he led me from the car into the building. I'm a firm believer in the fact that suits should be renewed at least every two years and that fashion should be painful only to the wearer, not the innocent bystander. I often decided instantly whether I liked someone and my dislike could be unreasonably fierce. It was a vampire thing. The agent instantly went to the top of my 'this might give me indigestion' list, but I knew I'd better behave myself and try to get along with this 'suit' for the time being.

The first thing I told him was that I had to have a room without windows. With a very Gallic shrug, he obliged and took me to a windowless cell in the basement. It dawned on me that they'd probably had no intention of giving me a room with a view in the first place. Although it was already late, everyone involved agreed that we should have our first interview there and then. A second man joined us, introducing himself as Pierre Leblanc. He was much younger than Jean-Claude, of medium height and rather skinny which, with along his badly cut, sandy-coloured hair and gold-rimmed glasses, led me to think he must have been hired for his brain rather than his brawn. I wondered what his skills were. *Have they hired a paranormal expert? Is he the French version of Agent Mulder?*

They led me to a small room with a mirrored wall and left me there for, I guessed, about half an hour. I knew they were observing me from the other side, so I took off my shirt and gave them something to look at. Even though I couldn't see my own reflection, I pretended to admire myself striking some impressive bodybuilding poses. I'd recognised their

2

conservative male type and knew they would not be amused. After half an hour they came in carrying digital recording equipment. Jean-Claude signalled to me to put my shirt back on and they sat down and switched their little machine on.

'For the record, please state your name and your date and place of birth,' Jean-Claude started.

I smiled. *Here we go!* 'My name is Cameron Blair. I was born in Edinburgh on 3 December 1895.'

I sat back to watch their expressions. Jean-Claude rolled his eyes and shifted impatiently in his chair, I could sense an outburst along the lines of 'Don't waste our bloody time you impertinent little prick' brewing, so I quickly asked them, 'Look behind you gentlemen.'

Their glances flicked from each other back to me before Pierre slowly turned around. It took a few seconds for him to understand what he saw, or rather, what he didn't see. He took in his own reflection and then got up to double check that I had none. Jean-Claude got up from his seat as well. They were clearly unsettled and I could almost see their brains whirring away trying to find a rational explanation.

'How do you *do* that?' Pierre spoke at last.

'I don't *do* anything. My reflection has just disappeared over the years. Now, I think it's time we discussed dinner arrangements.' I thought it best to get to the difficult – but crucial – part first.

Caught off-guard by the switch in direction, an unsuspecting Jean-Claude asked, distractedly, 'What would you like to eat, Monsieur Blair?' The penny hadn't even begun to drop yet.

'Yorkshire terrier, if you have any. Please.'

There was a moment of incredulity at the fact I'd requested a small lap dog for my dinner before Jean-Claude banged the table with his fist and cried, 'Is this all a big joke to you, you murdering scumbag?'

'Gentlemen, gentlemen!' I was enjoying this! 'You must have cottoned on by now that I am *not normal*! Sooner or later the uncomfortable subject of feeding me is going to come up. I'd like to discuss this as soon as possible; I get a *bit* tetchy when I'm hungry.'

They were being quite obtuse and refusing to see what was (not) in front of them so I thought it best to bring up another subject and let the understanding sink in slowly.

'Have you released George Baxter yet?'

They were taken aback by another abrupt change in the conversation's direction. I imagined they were trying to work out just how unstable I was and what kind of sociopathic tendencies I really had.

'He will be released tomorrow morning. We'll set up a telephone call with his daughter to confirm this with you. That will be the last contact you have with the outside world,' said Jean-Claude, relieved to be back on familiar territory and fully back in professional policeman mode.

What? No outside contact… but… What about Facebook and the chatrooms! What about the internet! I had agreed for them to fake my death, so I knew there couldn't be any virtual sightings of me, but the reality of what was coming hit me suddenly and hard.

'So what exactly do you like to eat, Monsieur Blair?' Pierre began carefully, perhaps trying a psychological approach and indulging my ravings.

I knew he wouldn't believe the answer, or really want to know the truth when he finally did grasp it, but I had to tell them. 'I drink blood, of course, like all vampires' I stated, matter of factly. 'For a while I will be ok on animal blood, as

4

long as it's fresh. But no bloody cats, please!'

'This is all a lot of bullshit, Monsieur Blair!' cried Jean-Claude. 'I will find out how you do this reflection trick and you will eat what we bring you.' Again, he brought his fist down hard on the table – his capacity for self-expression seemed quite limited.

I decided to be equally non-verbal and conclusive. I leapt out of my chair and over the table, knocking Jean-Claude and his chair to the ground and pinning him to the floor by the throat. When I had his full attention, I sprang my fangs inches from his face.

'Still think it is bullshit, Monsieur Bernard?' I asked coldly.

Pierre suddenly leapt into action and did his best to pull me off his colleague, but his weedy frame was no match for my strength. He quickly ran to the alarm button and rang for backup. I let go of the man and walked back to my chair just before three more agents burst in to find the suspect in his seat and Jean-Claude warily watching me and rubbing his throat. Without another word, all five men left the room.

I had no doubt they were all standing behind the mirror talking about what had just happened, but I was left by myself for a long time and I started to get bored. There was nothing in the room other than the three chairs, a metal table and the recording device. I decided to mess with the device as I was sure that would have them jogging back in.

Just as I don't have a reflection, I can't be recorded in any way, not on film and not on tape. The recorder made me think about some of the conversations I'd had with George over the years. Even though he had known me for a long time he still had issues with my vampireness and was always trying to catch me out. One morning he'd shown up with some equipment he had borrowed from a friend so he could be sure

I hadn't tinkered with it ahead of time.

'Ok Cameron, let's take your picture,' he'd said pointing a camera lens at me.

'Give it up, George. I can't be photographed,' I'd replied trying to ignore him.

'Aha! But this is digital!' he'd said, triumphant. 'There's no reason why I can't record your image this way!'

'I died nearly a hundred years ago, but here I am walking and talking to you. Stop trying to make sense of me, George. Some things just can't be explained.'

I'd become bored of going through this. We'd been here before when George was convinced there was no reason that sunlight should burn me to a crisp. He'd made me stick my hand out into the sun to prove it, and the bastard had been utterly without compassion as he'd watched my hand sizzle and blister in the morning light. 'Have you tried it with factor 50?' he'd asked, grinning, but he'd remained a very safe distance away out in the sunlight.

'You have a physical presence, therefore the laws of physics have to apply to you!' he'd continued stubbornly.

'Then take it up with Einstein and leave me alone,' was my retort.

'I can talk to you on the phone, so how can't I get a digital recording of you?' He'd got quite annoyed with me for not conforming to scientific rules.

'George, if you don't fuck off right this minute, I'll turn you into a vampire and you can go and bother yourself with all those questions!' I'd had enough and my head had started to hurt from all the physics mumbo-jumbo George had hit me with. Fortunately, he knew me well enough not to push any further and he and his equipment had beaten a hasty retreat, but afterwards I'd spotted him a few times retrieving the

6

recorder from some hidden location. He'd tried to capture my voice secretly, but never managed it of course.

Now, here I was sitting with another one of these gizmos in front of me, knowing the DCRI would do no better than George had.

I played around with the buttons on the recorder for a while and then the door opened as expected. They'd no doubt think I had done something to the device and managed to erase only *my* voice from the recording. They'd be scratching their heads wondering how I'd done it. Little things like that do amuse me!

Pierre and Jean-Claude came back into the room and I saw they had brought two Taser guns with them. They requested that I be handcuffed to the table and I agreed. I knew these measures would be insufficient – they'd both be dead in seconds if I wanted it so.

'Monsieur Blair, we will see if we can get a live animal for you tomorrow. Will that be ok?' Jean-Claude asked, on his guard now and closely observing my every move. They might not yet be fully on board with what I was, but they were clearly rattled enough to play along.

'Fine. Dog, cow, sheep and goats are all palatable.'

Then they resumed the business of taking my details and I told them the story of how I'd died and how I'd become a vampire. I explained how I had been wounded in the First World War and turned on the battlefield by a German vampire. There were still sceptical looks on the faces of the two agents, but they listened intently. They knew I was a dangerous individual who had killed at least once. To humour this psychopath with a vampire complex was to them, I thought, a price worth paying; they knew that in amongst the mad ravings there would be important information.

We didn't talk for long. It was late and it had been an eventful interview for the two agents. I was led back to my cell where I tried to settle in and adjust to my new life.

Chapter 2: Ginger

I had packed a few spy novels and my laptop, and though I was denied access to the internet they did allow me to use my computer. With their being the secret service, I didn't hold out much hope of finding an unsecured network. I was worried that the boredom would be a problem and determined to bring it up in our next interview. I'd been given a small cell with a metal bed, a tiny metal desk, a small metal wardrobe and two shelves. Everything was painted grey. I tried to make myself comfortable, but it wasn't easy in such hard and cold surroundings. I spent most of what was left of the first night folding and refolding my clothes so they fitted neatly in the wardrobe. The rest of my belongings were arranged tidily on the shelves.

When I was done I sat on the bed and looked around the small cell. *Was my friendship with a human really worth being locked up like this?* I had lost everything, my boat, some very fine clothes and a lot of money, but as with any big decision there is always more than one reason for making it. In the last few days before I'd decided to hand myself in, I'd felt something I hadn't felt before: fatigue. It had become a daily struggle to find food and shelter without being detected and in a way it might be good to have a roof over my head and let someone else take care of the logistics. It might not deliver Armani and champagne-soaked lovelies, but it would be easy.

I felt tired and defeated, but I reminded myself that I was doing a noble thing. The final reason that made me accept my surroundings for the moment was a boyish wish to be a secret agent. When Sean Connery had hit the silver screen as James

Bond, I'd imagined it could be me. *I have the looks and the accent!* I'd just have to convince the French agents that they were lucky to have me at their side. I lay back on the bed daydreaming about being parachuted behind enemy lines in the dead of night and the imaginary carnage put me in a better mood. I was optimistic that I could make the best of the situation I had voluntarily walked into.

At about 7am , I heard my cell door opening. A guard came in with a breakfast tray. I told him to take it away again as I couldn't eat anything other than blood.

'They told me you might say that,' he said, 'but I'm instructed to leave the food anyway.' He put the tray down on the desk. As he went to leave, I blocked his exit and held him back with my gaze.

'Firstly, you'll pick that tray back up, otherwise it'll go where the sun don't shine. Then you're going to tell those idiots outside that I don't have time to play their tedious game. I can't take anything other than blood.'

'Fine,' the man said, quickly, evidently not keen on confrontation with this unhinged prisoner.

They must have put their heads together after that and decided to humour me, maybe out of sheer curiosity to see what would happen. At around 11 o'clock the door opened and Pierre came in with a small dog on a leash, a scruffy-looking thing with coarse ginger fur. I assumed it was a stray they'd picked up from a dog shelter. The dog's fate had probably been sealed one way or another before I even walked into the DCRI headquarters.

'Can it stay with me? If you people feed him and walk him, he should last me a few days,' I told a very uncomfortable looking Pierre. *Entertainment and food! Result!*

'I suppose he can,' he said looking at the dog. He was

grasping the leash with both hands, not sure what to do.

I got up and took the leash from him and said, 'You might want to wait outside until I've had my breakfast.'

Pierre nodded and left me with the dog. I had the distinct impression that I was being watched, but I didn't mind, I wanted them to see me feed. I had just half a pint and the dog didn't make a sound or even struggle. He just stood there afterwards and looked at me with big mournful eyes. Probably no human had ever been much kinder to this creature. I stroked its scruffy little head and decided to name him Ginger, rather too cheerful a name for such a miserable looking dog but maybe the mutt would liven up if it had name we could call him by. I promised him I would demand a tennis ball.

I knocked on the door and told Pierre I was ready for whatever they had in store for me and added that Ginger would like a tennis ball.

Pierre looked relieved, probably because he hadn't walked in to find a furry bloodbath, he just nodded and the dog was entrusted to a junior agent. I was led back to the same spartan interview room of the night before where I was once again cuffed to the table. I could see they'd brought their Taser guns back with them. The recording device was switched on and Pierre and Jean-Claude seated themselves in front of me. It would probably take them a few days to figure out there was little point in recording the interviews, apart from any use there might be in taping their own voices. I sat smiling innocently in my chair, ready for their questions. At this point I was still keen to talk to them; after all I'm an interesting guy with a lot of great stories!

'So. We've established that you became a vampire in 1915,' started Jean-Claude, with barely disguised sarcasm. 'I assume

11

you have killed many people between then and the murder of Yvette Jaunet. We would, of course, like to help the police solve some of these crimes.'

I nodded my agreement.

'We'd like to start with the murder of Mademoiselle Jaunet. We'll then check out your account and if all is satisfactory, arrange for the release of Monsieur Baxter,' continued Jean-Claude.

It was the murder of Yvette Jaunet that had landed me in this mess in the first place. I had got by for years funding a lavish lifestyle by burgling houses and stealing jewellery without getting caught. Over time, my lust for luxury had grown, culminating in the purchase of a luxury yacht that I had moored in Cannes. It was at a party there that I had met socialite Yvette and noticed her fabulous emerald jewellery.

I could have thought longer and harder about how to commit the perfect crime, but to be perfectly frank, I'm not that bright and killing to cover my tracks is sometimes just a lot easier. It was only because of the arrest of my fence, Rashid, that the authorities had caught on to me after they'd found some of Yvette's jewellery in his possession. There were some emails between Rashid and me, so I knew it wouldn't take the authorities long to uncover me as a possible suspect.

When I'd learned of Rashid's arrest I'd fled, but George, who worked for me, had chosen to stay behind. He was innocent and I'd believed he had nothing to worry about. Unfortunately, during the police search of my yacht, some of Yvette's dog's DNA had been found on George's shoe: he had disposed of the dog's body knowing nothing of the murder. It had been a Yorkshire terrier, one of my favourite snacks and I hadn't been able to resist taking this little morsel from the crime scene back to my yacht. George was used to finding the aftermath of my food binges and thought nothing of it. No lover of animals, he had dumped the body overboard and cleaned up the mess.

I made myself comfortable and told the agents about the murder in as much detail as I could, now and then demonstrating my body's position in relation to hers so they could check the forensics and establish without doubt that it was me that had committed the crime. When I was done, they stopped the recording and handed the memory card to a junior agent, I assumed to have the recordings typed up and sent off for comparison. A new memory card was inserted and we continued.

'We would like to talk now about some of your other crimes, mainly any other murders you may have committed,' Jean-Claude said, looking serious and professional. 'The problem is that these crimes were committed many years ago, or so I assume, as you are claiming to be 118 though you look more like a 23-year-old.'

I nodded my head in agreement again. *Not my problem mate!*

'While we would like to be as thorough as we can, I don't think there is much point in discussing anything that happened before 1960,' continued Jean-Claude.

'I was in London then. Do you still want to know who I killed?' I asked wracking my brains for memories of who and when. It was a bit of a blur and I couldn't be sure if I would provide accurate information.

'When did you return to France, Monsieur Blair?' asked Pierre.

'1977. And can we cut the Monsieur shit? I'm Cameron. Please.'

The title 'Mr Blair' made me think of my father, a respectable honest man with a family. I was none of these things and it annoyed me no end when anyone addressed me as Mr or Monsieur.

'OK, Cameron. Let's get started in 1977,' said Jean-Claude. 'Can you remember all your murders since then?'

The assumption that I had committed so many murders I might not remember them all ticked me off, but as he was right I decided to ignore the insult and co-operate.

'I do remember all my murders, as a matter of fact. Some with great fondness,' I said, sounding full of confidence. But that diminished quickly once I set off down memory lane. *What the hell was I up to in 1977?* I thought long and hard, going back in time to my first days in Nice. Happy memories of meeting backpackers and enjoying the warm summer night air. I didn't remember killing anyone in 1977 as food was plentiful and life was cheap. Then, slowly, a memory washed back into my head! *Fuck, yes! The jeweller!*

I started by talking about my farm in England – one of my less than brilliant ventures. Living in the countryside and being self-sufficient had seemed like such a good idea, but the quiet of the countryside was not for me and I certainly wasn't cut out for the hard work that a farm with livestock entailed. So, after an unpleasant winter, I'd decided to move to the south of France. I talked about my arrival in Nice and gave details of the apartment I had lived in until 1984.

I had taken up my old, trusted trade as a burglar again and after only a few weeks I had an impressive stash of jewellery that I needed to offload. I'd stalked several dodgy-looking jewellers that sold second-hand jewellery until I was convinced I'd found one I could do business with. On a mild winter's night I decided to make first contact. I walked into a small shop in a backstreet of Nice and found a friendly, dark-haired man with a moustache, behind the counter. I told him I had some jewellery to sell and he agreed to have a look at it. I put about five pieces before him – not the best ones, as I wanted to see if he offered me a good price for the average stuff first. He asked me where I had got the pieces and I said as vaguely as possible that they were family heirlooms and that there may be more to come.

After looking them over, he said his cousin would also have to look at the pieces before he could buy them, as they ran the business together. He asked me to wait while he made a phone call. As soon as I heard him talking, I realised that he was Armenian and that the supposed cousin was not a business partner but a policeman. When he hung up the phone I jumped on him and bit his neck, drinking just a little, and then I quickly snapped his neck and disguised my bite marks with a couple of razor cuts. A broken neck and a cut throat might seem an unusual homicide but it wouldn't point to vampire activity. I made a quick exit, taking as much jewellery as I could fit in my bag. I could just have left the shop without killing him – at worst I'd have been on the radar of the Nice police for dealing in stolen goods – but I'd been miffed that the jeweller had tried to pull the wool over my eyes. The shop stock had been an added bonus.

With one story complete, the two agents turned off the recording machine and left the room, probably to check what I'd given them against the old case file. It had made the front page of the local news as it had been such a violent murder and robbery, but I don't think the Nice police had ever come close to solving it. I'd been a little wary afterwards, as the murder of a colleague would have put all the dealers on edge and I was sure lists of the stolen stock would be doing the rounds. My stash would have been too hot to handle. I had managed to sell the gent's watches I'd taken to some unsuspecting backpackers, telling my 'fellow travellers' that I had run out of money and needed to sell my watch. The rest of the jewellery had been more difficult, so I'd decided to try my luck in Marseilles, a city with a tough criminal underbelly.

I'd soon run into trouble with a Corsican gang. I'd thought I could do what had been so successful in London where I would walk into a backstreet pub in a rundown area and start a fight, beat or cut up a few heavies and end up on the payroll of a criminal Mr Big impressed with my prowess. The Marseille fight had gone well. Two big Corsicans pulled some knives on me and blood was shed – mainly theirs – and when I'd licked the razor, it wasn't fear I'd seen in their eyes. Rather, it was intense hatred. These guys had not liked their arses being handed to them by some kid with a Parisian accent, and I'd had to make a hasty exit when they started coming after me with a shotgun. I'd soon realised that people down in the south didn't like my northern accent. I'd lived in Paris, and eaten Parisians, for too long; I had to switch to local cuisine to be able to blend in.

When the two agents came back in neither looked over the moon.

'I'm not sure what you did with the device but for some reason it's only recording our voices,' said Jean-Claude.

'Really? That's odd.' I feigned surprise.

'One of our agents typed up the transcripts of the last sessions so we'll leave you in your cell to write in your answers,' said Pierre.

What? Homework? No way! That was not how it was supposed to go.

'The reason my voice isn't on the tapes is the same as the one that means I can't be caught on CCTV, X-ray and a whole array of electronic capturing devices,' I said, resigned. Our wee game may have ended, but I was damned if I was going to sit and write all my answers down. I like to *tell* a good story, but writing it down isn't much fun at all! I'd left school at 14 and been glad to do so. Sitting still for hours on end and writing had been torture for me, even when I was a human child. Since I had become a vampire, I was even more restless. The agents looked at each other and Jean-Claude let out a deep sigh.

'I've talked to you on the phone, so there is no reason I can see why we can't record you.'

I felt my heart sink. I can't explain why things are the way they are, I just know they are.

'I don't know *why* you can't do it, but trust me, you can't. But by all means get another machine in here,' I added forcefully. 'I'll be damned if I'm writing up my answers!'

Jean-Claude sighed. 'Right, we'd better find a stenographer for our next session then.'

I was relieved that, for once, I had been taken at my word. One theory George had come up with was that only people and animals could perceive me. I was dead, I needed their blood to exist, and maybe without their presence I'd just be a ghost, *one that can burgle your house and walk out with your valuables.*

For the rest of the day and night, I was left in my cell and I worked away on my statement adding little drawings here and there. I thought the statement needed some colour, but I'd only been given a black ballpoint. They'd provided a tennis ball for the dog, but he showed little interest in it. I let him sleep on my bed and amused myself with trying to get the ball into the wastepaper basket.

***

The next morning, the two agents were joined by a stenographer. He was introduced briefly as Laurent Goldman and I was told he usually worked as a court reporter. It was explained to me that Laurent was filled in on the unusual nature of these interviews and that he'd had to sign some papers saying he was at no point to breathe a word of what was going on here to anyone. I observed Laurent; he looked nervous and was trying not to stare at me. I had no such hesitation, which put him even more on edge. He looked to be around 30, with rather angelic blond, curly hair and soft features. Not the type, I thought, to be exposed to the gruesome crimes we were about to detail. I watched him as they laid a few photos out before me. He flinched at the sight of a dead man and bent over his machine, starting to tap away even before anyone even spoke.

'Is this the jeweller you killed?' asked Jean-Claude, pointing to the photo of a man lying on the floor with a puddle of blood under his head.

'Yep, looks like the guy.' It had been a long time ago, but I vaguely remembered him. 'What are you going to do with this case?'

'Probably nothing, as it doesn't look as though anyone was wrongfully convicted. The case is too old and closed,' Jean-Claude stared at me for a while, probably wondering how I knew the details of an obscure murder that had happened in the 1970s, years before the young man he saw in front of him was even born. Lost in thought, he packed the papers away.

I'd lain low for a couple of years after the jeweller's murder, resorting to pickpocketing again as that didn't need a fence. By the 1980s I had found a reliable and suitably criminal contact and we'd done business together for many years.

'So you guys ready for the next murder?' I asked merrily. The two agents exchanged glances and then they nodded.

I told them that, in my early days in the south, people hadn't taken kindly to my Parisian accent and divulged how I absorbed a victim's language by drinking his or her blood. One night in Toulon I'd spoken to some of the local prostitutes working the port area. I'd found one with a fantastic broad local accent and she'd agreed to get into my car. We'd driven to a deserted spot where she'd given me a rather good blow job, and then I'd had her for dinner. It had done wonders for my integration into Niçois life. I buried her body somewhere north of Toulon, but couldn't now remember where. A few days after I'd killed her, I'd spotted that she had been reported missing in the local paper, but I didn't think she'd ever been found. I'd disguised myself with some glasses and a wig and I'd driven a stolen car, so the descriptions doing the rounds hadn't lead back to me.

'You know I speak Afghan, which could be useful to you boys? I could listen in to Taliban chatter and translate for you,' I explained, already working on creating a new role for myself within the organisation.

'You speak Pashto or Dari? Afghanistan has many languages and even more dialects,' said Pierre, and I realised languages were his speciality.

'I don't know. I bit a few Taliban, so whatever they spoke,' I replied. The skill didn't come with labels. It was always later that you found out what national cuisine you had just sampled. I asked Pierre if he had been to Afghanistan and if he knew what they spoke near Kandahar. He confirmed that he had and we spoke for a while in Pashto, as Pierre claimed it was. We discussed the different tribes and dialects of Southern Afghanistan until Jean-Claude cut us short, irritated at our babbling on in a foreign language he didn't understand, and brought the interview back on track. I wondered how many languages I had picked up by now, it would be fun to find out.

They decided to pause for lunch and led me back to the cell. Pierre asked me to make a list of all the languages I knew I spoke. I was happy to have something to do. The little dog just wanted to sleep so I had it lying next to me on the bed. I got to a total of about 18 languages, but there might've been more.

After lunch we carried on for a few hours more, going over the report on the prostitute I had killed and trying to pinpoint where I had buried her. We looked at Google Earth to see if any of the scenery looked familiar and I wracked my brains to remember that night. With some maps and photos I thought I might be able to narrow it down to about ten square kilometres for them, but it would still be some task to find a 35-year-old corpse in that terrain.

At the end of the day they confirmed that my story about Yvette's murder had checked out and they were going to release George. They led me to my cell and told me I would receive a call later. In the end they didn't let me talk to George or Emmy and I just received a video recording of both of them standing outside somewhere in Grasse saying they were fine. George looked older than I remembered; prison can't have been easy on him even though he was one of the toughest people I knew. Emmy looked stunning as usual, cheeks all rosy in the early spring sun and her long, blonde hair framing her pretty face. Both thanked me for turning myself in and wished me well. Suddenly, I felt very lonely and cut off. Full realisation that my life would be very hard from now on was slowly dawning.

Chapter 3: Valerie

We carried on the next day when they wanted to know about my third murder in France since 1977, which had happened sometime in the early 1980s. I was still following British fashion and trends and the people I hung out with were from all over Europe, so it was taking me a while to adjust fully to local life. I had broken into a smart villa overlooking Nice and the Baie des Anges and discovered that it belonged to a British family. While there were disappointingly few items of value, as it was probably a second home, I'd been delighted to find a stack of *Smash Hits* in one of the kids' bedrooms. I was bowled over by the pictures of all the bands they featured and with my dark hair and pale complexion totally fancied myself as a New Romantic poster boy. Unlike Adam Ant, I really *was* a dandy highwayman: robbing, stealing and of course looking fabulous whilst doing it.

I'd started dressing in big, eighteenth-century-style white shirts and stripy pirate trousers. I found some amazing shiny black, knee-high boots and even broke into a museum as their brochure featured a rather fancy Hussar's jacket that I thought would look dashing. I took the sword too but never wore it in public. I wanted to wear eyeliner and have big hair with lots of gel and hairspray, but that was a huge problem to achieve with the vampire lack of reflection thing. I'd often thought it was very cruel to deny a vain creature like myself the pleasure of looking at himself in a mirror.

The whole New Romantics fashion hadn't quite caught on in Nice and I would have looked very out of place if I'd dressed as flamboyantly as I wanted to, so I'd been surprised in a club one night when I spotted a tall woman who shared my aesthetic. She looked amazing, with striking make-up and big, blonde hair full of colourful ribbons. I went over to talk to her and discovered we had more than fashion sense in common: she was from Dundee and a fellow Scot. She told me her parents had a house in Nice and that she'd needed to get away from Dundee for a while.

'People can be cruel, you know? Here, I can be myself.' I saw tears welling up in her eyes. I hadn't lived in Scotland for over 80 years and was disappointed to hear that you couldn't be fashion forwards in my home country. In many ways, I suppose I was still very naïve.

We went on to have a good laugh though, and chatted away for hours. She looked amazing, but I didn't fancy her. She was tall and blonde, but not what you would call pretty. She didn't make a move on me either and when it got to closing time I asked her if she would come and do my hair and make-up for a night out sometime. Valerie, as I'd discovered she was called, agreed and I gave her my address and asked her to meet me there the following Friday night.

When she arrived the next week, it became a lot clearer in the cold light of my hallway why Valerie had wanted to leave Dundee. I spotted the Adam's apple and beard stubble pushing its way through a thick layer of make-up. I was curious and wanted to know everything about him, always fascinated by people pretending to be something other than what they were. While he did my hair and make-up, Valerie told me how he'd never felt comfortable in his skin as a boy. He'd often suffered beatings because he was different to the other boys and it only got worse when he began to wear make-up at the age of 16. Once he'd left school at 18, which was about a year before we met, he'd decided to dress and live as a woman full-time, but friends and family hadn't taken it well. He'd started to take hormones and eventually, wanting to make the decision final, had found a clinic in Morocco that would do the operation. I couldn't imagine having my male bits cut off, but then again I'd never wanted to be a woman. I thought she was very brave. She wanted me to have a look at the handiwork but I hurriedly stopped her pulling a mirror from her bag and explained it by telling her I had a few issues of my own. She shrugged her shoulders and put all her brushes and combs away. Then we took her little, green Triumph Spitfire into town and attracted the desired amount of attention as we strutted into a nightclub.

As Valerie drove me home at the end of the night, we were in high spirits, laughing and dishing out catty comments about the other club goers. When we got to my flat, Valerie leaned in, pulled me into her arms and planted her lips forcefully on mine. It wasn't a gentle or tender kiss and often, when I get surprised, my fangs push out. I cut her lip before I could retract them. When I tasted the blood, I got excited and the vampire in me took over, pushing reason aside. I heard myself panting 'Come up to my flat!' and we ran upstairs and headed straight for the bedroom. She pushed me on the bed and got on top of me kissing me and tearing at my clothes. I felt like a rabbit caught in the headlights not knowing what to do with my hands, but I was also a very happy and turned on bunny, because Valerie certainly did know. She, more than any girl I'd ever met, knew what to do with the male anatomy. With a surprised scream, I came and lay back, spent and somewhat bewildered.

'Thank you,' she whispered, kissing my naked stomach.

No thank you, dear girl, (boy?)! My god, what just happened?

'Why are you thanking me?' I asked.

'Not many people accept me as I am. You were kind,' she replied, resting her head on my chest.

I'd been anything but kind! The prospect of dinner had swept me along. 'Do you want some water, Valerie?' I asked getting up.

She nodded and I went into the kitchen to find some glasses, water and a sleeping tablet. Valerie was sitting on the bed when I went back into the bedroom, and I handed her the water with the crushed up tablet in it and got into bed.

'Stay,' I said tapping the space beside me.

She stripped to her underwear but wasn't comfortable revealing more of the body she was so desperately unhappy with. She fell asleep with full make-up on and I fed and looked at her sleeping. I knew I was playing with fire, stringing her along and giving her the hope of a relationship. I didn't want any emotional attachments as they hadn't worked out too well in the past. I was a vampire and relations with humans were always complicated, yet she did intrigue me and we'd had tremendous fun together.

I woke her up at about ten o'clock. 'I need to get ready for work Valerie. Do you mind leaving?'

She didn't and got dressed straight away, leaving without a fuss or a word. If I were not to seek contact, she'd probably think I regretted our night together and that would be that, but I found I didn't want to leave it at that. I had enjoyed our time getting dressed up and going out together. I badly wanted a friend, someone who shared my tastes and background, but I did not want a girlfriend so I needed to take a step back. I phoned her a few nights later and asked her over to my place.

'I don't have any regrets, Valerie, but I'm not ready for a relationship,' I began, once she had sat down. 'I just had a bad break up and there are a lot of issues to sort out. To be honest I'm not sure I'm completely over her,' I lied, melancholically.

Valerie looked at her feet. I could see she was used to her romances not having happy endings.

'Can we go back to being friends?' I asked.

She nodded her head, probably hoping she would win me over eventually, and we agreed to meet once a week to go out to a club. She loved doing hair and make-up and, being new to Nice, hadn't made many friends yet. While I didn't think Nice was any more tolerant than Dundee at the time, there was an advantage in not being known and in the right light she could pass for female. I thought the friendship would be able to endure for a while once we'd taken the sex out of it, but one night on leaving the club and walking back to the car we found our route blocked by three young men.

'Where do you two nancy boys think you're going?' said one, as all three moved in menacingly.

I saw a knife flash out of the corner of my eye and I pushed Valerie behind me and out of the way. I always relished a good fight, especially if blood was likely to flow so without a second thought I jumped on the guy with the knife and easily disarmed him. After the first few cuts I lost myself and the red haze only lifted when I heard Valerie scream, 'Cameron stop! Please stop!'

I was covered in blood and still had the knife in my hand. One guy was on the pavement, moaning and holding his side, the other two stood looking shocked, their backs against the wall and showing signs of cuts and bruises. They picked up their injured mate and dragged him away as quickly as they could. Valerie was a blubbering mess and I led her quickly to the car, drove to my apartment and asked if she wanted to come upstairs. She had calmed down a little by then, but could barely look at me. She was clearly distressed by the bloodstains on my shirt and told me she just wanted to get home.

The next day I read in the local paper that three men had been attacked by a gang of men and that one had succumbed to his severe injuries. I was pleased the men had lied in their statements. *Too embarrassed to admit you all got beaten up by one baby-faced nancy boy!* I called Valerie from a phone box that night and she assured me she wouldn't contact the police. She'd been there and knew it was self-defence, albeit rather vigorous, but having heard that one of the men had died, she didn't want to see me again. She started to cry and hung up sobbing 'goodbye!'.

Damn, letting women into my life was always a bad idea, even when they were men!

After the fight, I got out of town for a while and looked up young George in London. I killed someone there too, but the French agents didn't need to know about that.

'So, *technically* it wasn't murder, but perhaps it was a tad too vigorous on the self defence front!' I said cheerfully. The men didn't share my mirth and Pierre told me sombrely that we would have a break.

The agents left to go and check the dates I had given them. They had allowed me to bring my laptop into the room, and I was relieved that they were beginning to realise that I got dangerously bored very quickly. When they came back in, they told me that this case had also been closed a long time before with no conviction made. Then they asked me about my work with George and about the hostages we had rescued.

My usefulness in the hostage rescue business had probably been the only reason George tolerated me. He'd been in the army and was SAS trained. When he left, he'd wanted to do something worthwhile with his skills and thought I should too. Unlike him, it was only the payoff we received from the rescued hostages' families – and the often deliciously bloody rescues – that motivated me. I was pleased they wanted to know about this, as there were a number of French hostages being held at that time and I was champing at the bit to get out in the world again. Maybe they would see their way to using me.

However, I came to realise over the next few weeks that they were far from ready to let me loose. First, they wanted to know absolutely *everything* about me.

Chapter 4: Laurent

'You know, I really don't kill that much – on average about one every five years or so. I think I've been rather restrained for a vampire!'

I hadn't liked their tone when they asked me about the fourth murder. It had been a bad night and start of the day and I wasn't in the mood to talk. The scruffy, straggly dog had consistently refused to play with the tennis ball and just wanted to lie in a corner and sleep. I'd found him dead that morning before I could have my breakfast.

'You guys have to do better than that. One manky dog is *not* going to keep me satisfied for long. Just get a few cows in here!' I ranted. The agents assured me they would look into doing so, but right now they wanted to get back to business.

'I'm not starting before I've had something to eat!' I made sure my eyes gave them clear warning of the impending danger.

Jean-Claude really disliked that this suspect dictated things to him. I could detect the utter disgust in his eyes when I talked about needing to feed and I saw how he judged me when I spoke of the people I'd killed. He hated the fact that I had no remorse. Deep down, I think he still didn't believe I was a vampire. To him I was just an utterly despicable human. In return, I hated his cheap nylon suits, bad haircut and moral judgement. The man despised me and the feeling was mutual.

'We're *trying* to get you something, but you'll have to be patient,' he said.

His superior tone tipped me over the edge. Violent hatred welled up in me and there was no stopping it. I snapped the chain on my handcuffs, sprang over the table and planted my fangs in Jean-Claude's neck. I heard the Taser gun going off but felt little more than a tingling sensation. Pierre flung open the door and shouted for help. I let go and went back to my chair, licking my lips like the cat that got the cream. I smiled coldly at the terrified Jean-Claude, who was holding a handkerchief to his neck. Laurent stood with his back to the wall and I'm sure if I'd moved towards him he'd have wet his trousers. When the full gun squad charged in and shouted at me to get down on the floor, Laurent bolted from the room and that was the last I saw of him.

'Awww, c'mon! I was just getting myself a dash of breakfast seeing as you lot failed to provide,' I protested. 'The man's fine! A little blood donation never harmed anyone, so don't get your knickers in a twist!'

They were ranged around me pointing their guns nervously in my direction, but I remained sitting in my chair looking as calm and harmless as could be. Having just eaten, I wasn't too keen to get down on the floor. *It might give me indigestion.* 'If you guys play nice, I will be as sweet as can be, but just be aware I could kill you all before you even got a shot off.'

They retreated and locked me in the room. I had fed and felt relaxed so I switched on my computer to play a few games. After three hours alone, I became troubled. *What are they up to?* I began to regret my impulsive behaviour and became worried that I might have brought about the exact opposite of what I was trying to achieve. I wanted them to jump to my demands, get me cows, dogs and game consoles. Instead I might have lost their trust and co-operation forever. Incarceration was not agreeing with me and I felt like a trapped tiger. *Yes, it's fun attacking the zookeepers, but they'll never let you out of your cage now!* I paced up and down in the small room, thinking hard about how I could turn the situation around.

A light came on behind the mirror and illuminated three men in an adjoining room. They must have flicked a switch that turned the mirror in my interview room into clear glass. I could hear them as well, when they wanted me to. Pierre and Jean-Claude were there but the third man was new. He introduced himself as Benjamin Estrosi the head of the department. He was a few years younger than Jean-Claude and had a full head of curly black hair, kept in check with a good haircut and some product. He wore a pair of fashionable glasses and his suit, whilst not new, was better quality than the garbage Jean-Claude wore. Even before he told me, I knew he was the boss.

'Monsieur Blair, the kind of behaviour you exhibited earlier will not be tolerated again. Any further injuries to my agents will result in severe repercussions. We're very close to putting you down, like the savage animal that you are!' He emphasised each word by tapping on the window with his index finger.

'C'mon! I only had half a pint!' I said amicably. 'I bet Jean-Claude's feeling no worse than he did this morning. But I'll be a pussycat from now on...' *Ha ha! And we all know how vile cats can be!*

'We will also not tolerate being threatened or dictated to,' Estrosi continued.

Exasperated, I had to get my side across. 'Look. I'm *not human*! You can't just give me a sandwich and expect me to be happy. You have to understand that I'm a vampire and I have different needs.'

'We *do* understand that and we are in the process of getting you food and materials to keep you occupied, but *you* have to understand that it takes time. We've not dealt with your kind before.'

'I don't think my demands are particularly tricky. There are hundreds of stray dogs awaiting execution if they can't be rehomed. What does a dog from a shelter cost these days? About 120 or 130 euros? I imagine I'm actually quite cheap to maintain compared to a human prisoner.'

'But there are certain logistics to overcome. Most animal shelters don't hand out dogs willy-nilly, but we are working on it,' he assured me, curtly.

I suddenly had an idea of how to bring them back on side. *You live with evil to prevent a greater one.* 'You should also understand that I'm not the only one of my kind... There may well come a time when you need my help.'

I watched their expressions turn to horror and felt a weight lifting. I had them back on the hook! The agents deliberated outside the room for a while and when they came back in Estrosi laid out how things would proceed from now on. Further interviews would be conducted by agents from the safety of the adjoining room and I would be taken to and from my cell by heavily armed guards. They agreed to give me a telly and I would get the papers delivered daily. They also promised that they were sourcing both a PlayStation and another dog. I thanked them and, as a parting shot, told them Jean-Claude had made an excellent breakfast so I would be fine for a day or so.

***

It took them until the late evening to find me something edible. At around ten o'clock my cell door was opened and a bleating goat was dragged in. I raised my eyebrows, but closed the door on the guards without a word. *Never had goat*

31

before. Who knows? It might be good. I looked at the little horned monster that was already nibbling away at my blanket. I quickly had dinner and knocked on the door.

'I think I'd prefer a dog. This thing here is eating my bed,' I told them, handing the guard the rope that was around the beast's neck. 'Here. He's your problem now.'

'Was he edible?' asked the guard. Gaston, I think he was called. He was a few years older than some of the other guards, but I liked him as he was calm and not unfriendly.

'It was alright. I don't want it living in my cell though!'

'I'll bring him back tomorrow,' Gaston said, patting the goat's side.

I shrugged my shoulders at that, hoping this would be a temporary solution and they were working on getting me a dog.

It took them a few days to find a new stenographer as Laurent hadn't wanted to return to the job. He was an outside contractor so they couldn't force him. Finally, everything was set to continue and I was led back into the interview room by my armed guards. Three men were waiting behind the armoured glass in the adjoining room, thinking they were safe. The new stenographer was introduced as Didier Constantin. He was much older than Laurent and looked less nervous. I guessed he wasn't far off retirement age; he already had the short grey hair and bland attire of a pensioner, beige trousers and a beige and green checked shirt. I couldn't see them but I suspected some sensible rubber-soled shoes completed the drab outfit. I wondered if I would have ended up looking like that if I'd been allowed to grow old. *Good god! I might have taken up golf and lost all fashion sense!* I quickly shook off the vision of myself wearing plus fours and opened proceedings.

'So. It was, I think, in about 1987 that I killed this old battle-axe in Nice. It was in a detached bungalow in the Mont-Boron Area.'

That part of town had been a favourite haunt of mine at the time, as it was affluent and pickings could be rich. I had stalked a quiet street for a number of nights and noted a few potential target properties that had older residents. I decided to go for a place with a very frail looking old biddy, even though she didn't appear to have a dog. I mostly target houses with something to steal *and* a nice snack for later, but this lady wore a pearl necklace that looked expensive. I let myself in with my tools and was immediately confronted with a strange, unearthly bleating. Two pairs of demonic blue eyes in black faces approached and a furry devil launched itself at my legs and dug sharp claws into my flesh. I plucked it off and flung it against the wall with all my might. It seemed to stick for a moment, before dropping lifelessly to the floor. The other bleating demon lost its nerve and ran away. And then I felt a sharp, shooting pain in my back. When I turned round I saw a white-haired, wild-eyed harpy in a pink nightgown lifting her pale wrinkled arm to bring a knife down on me again. This time though, I was a step ahead of her and I grabbed her arm and twisted it behind her back as she struggled weakly. Her neck snapped as easily as a little bird's.

I had no sooner sat down in the hall, to compose myself for a moment, when demon number two had a go at me and tore its claws across my face. I grabbed it and hurled it too against the wall. Finally, the house was quiet and calm! I recognised the little demons as Siamese cats and hoped I would never encounter any of them again. At least the house had contained some worthwhile items and pieces. I'd been right about the old woman's necklace: the pearls were real and the clasp was diamond and sapphire. She also had a gold Cartier wristwatch and a couple of other decent gold pieces. I felt less silly making my way back to my apartment with cat scratches all over my face knowing I had a good haul. In any case, by the time I got home the wounds had healed. It confirmed my view yet again that all cats were evil, a view I'd held since 1916 when I'd made the mistake of biting into one.

I'd been hiding out on a farm in a haystack during my early days as a vampire, when suddenly I'd felt the straw move and a small creature worked its way towards me. It made itself comfortable on my stomach and I stroked it, grateful for its warmth. Then, without warning, it bit me, hissed and tried to get away. *Not so fast pussycat!* I dragged it back by its tail – it had just volunteered itself as lunch with its unprovoked attack and I sank my teeth vengefully into it as it struggled. Then I got the most unpleasant surprise! The blood tasted just *awful*. I dropped the cat immediately and it sprang away. As it was daytime, I couldn't go looking for something to rinse my mouth out with and I threw up a few times. I tried to rub the rotten putrid taste out of my mouth with straw, and then lay feeling nauseous and utterly sorry for myself until nightfall. Never again!

***

My tendency to digress when I'd had enough forced the agents to call it a day at about noon and two armed guards escorted me back to my cell. There, a large, golden dog and a PlayStation awaited me. I had managed to get some good stuff out of them, but I still felt I'd shot myself in the foot by behaving so badly. I knew they wouldn't trust me again for a good few months – if ever. I looked through the games they'd left and found most of them were quite old, but they'd still keep me occupied for a few days.

As I organised my new things and tidied my room, I began to feel uneasy. Something wasn't quite right. I knew someone must have been in my cell to drop off the PlayStation, but I began to notice that a few things were just ever so slightly out of place. They'd obviously searched my room. Then I noticed what was missing. *Fuck! They've taken my painting!* They'd said there would be repercussions and knowing the painting was important to me they were holding it hostage!

The picture had been painted by Hélène, a girl I had been very much in love with when I first came to Paris in the 1920s. She was human and I could never bring myself to tell her that I was a vampire. I still regret making that decision, as the secret between us tore her apart and she'd ended up committing suicide. I'd steered well clear of forming attachments with women ever since and would only spend one night with someone, often deliberately being quite unpleasant afterwards, knowing that it was kinder to them in the long run. The painting reminded me of how different I was and that I should be on my guard. It was one of the few personal items I'd kept with me and now they had taken it. I tore the *Financial Times* into tiny pieces to calm myself and stop the anger from building. Today really had turned into a very bad day.

I was left in my cell until the following morning by which time I felt like a little boy being punished for misbehaving, locked in his room to reflect on his 'attitude'.

Chapter 5: Blondie

'I hope you put that painting in a safe place!' I shot daggers at the men behind the glass. How dare they take the one thing I hadn't been able to let go of all these years? I'd carried it with me wherever I'd gone; it reminded me never to fall in love again. As much as I adored women, I was never going to let another one get as close to me as Hélène had.

I was angry, maybe as much at myself as at them because I'd thought long and hard about what to do with the painting before bringing it along with me. Once before, I'd hidden another painting in Paris' catacombs, but they were just too busy now to be a safe hiding place. And leaving it with a human... well, humans have a habit of not being eternal and I didn't know how soon I'd be back to collect it. Who knew what might happen in the meantime? A car crash, falling masonry; things happened to humans. So I had decided it was best to keep it with me. I regretted that decision now.

'You'll get it back for good behaviour, don't worry Cameron,' said Pierre.

I folded my arms in moody defiance.

'Cameron, you told us before that there are more of your kind. What can you tell us about them?' said Jean-Claude, getting on with what they really wanted to know. This was a matter of national security after all; the thought of vampires living amongst them, eating innocent French citizens had them terrified. I was mostly going to lie to them, as I didn't want to drop Nanette or Carl-Heinz – the only other vampires I actually knew – in it.

Carl-Heinz was my maker. I had been curious about him since he'd left me to my own devices on the battlefield of Loos in 1915. He had found me fighting for my life after I was shot, drained me of my last drops of blood and turned me into a creature like himself before abandoning me. I had been angry with him for years, as I'd had to figure out by myself what it meant to be a vampire, but I'd decided to trace him after I became a murder suspect. When I found him in Berlin we had become friends. I learned that he'd been imprisoned and experimented on for a long time. He had suffered enough and deserved to be free, so I wasn't going to tell them about him.

Nanette had spotted me on the Cannes party circuit and sussed me out. Although she'd wanted me gone then, she had warned me of Rashid's arrest so I could flee. There was still no love lost between us; she thought I was a womanising good-for-nothing and I, well frankly it *bothered* me that she didn't like me! Usually everybody liked me! I had an adorable, blue-eyed, baby face that melted most people's hearts. But not hers – she was cold even by vampire standards. The woman had even killed her own maker! I was the only one of her kind she knew though, and so an uneasy bond remained between us. Neither of us wanted the demise of the other.

Carefully selecting the details I could safely give them, I began 'Of course there would be the vampire that made me. That was in France in 1915, but I have felt his presence from time to time, mainly when I was in Paris.' That should keep them chasing their tails for a few days I thought confidently! I had been active in Paris and it was true I had felt another vampire there, but it wasn't anyone I knew, so I didn't care what they dragged up. It was likely to have been Otto, but from what I knew of him, he could take care of himself.

Otto was kind of my brother. He'd been captured as a human and placed in the same institution as Carl-Heinz who had then become his maker too. Unlike Carl-Heinz, Otto had been immune to the drugs they were giving the vampires to try to control them. Otto had pretended to be under their command, but bolted as soon as he saw an opportunity. According to Carl-Heinz, he had been the only one to escape the facility and I'd been sure it was him whose presence I had felt over the years. Carl-Heinz and I felt each other's presence too, but I knew he'd never been to France. Otto was clever and I wanted to believe he was still out there. I knew so little about him it wasn't likely I was giving anything away that would help the DCRI find him.

'When is the last time you felt this vampire?' asked Pierre.

'About 1933, I think.' That was a lie too. The last time I had felt something was in Nice in 1985, but I didn't want them to start vampire hunting in Nanette's neck of the woods.

'Any others?' asked Jean-Claude.

'What do you mean others, it's not like we grow on trees! Do you not have to go off and find this vampire? He might still be in Paris.'

'It's unlikely if the last time you sensed him was in 1933,' said Jean-Claude tersely. 'You said there were others of your kind so you'll have to give us something more than a vague sense of something 80 years ago.'

'Serge,' I said meekly. I had wanted to keep this story for another time, but I sensed a lot of scepticism from across the table and knew I needed to get them back with something that was at least partly true.

'Serge? You know this vampire?' asked Jean-Claude crossing his arms. 'I hope you have a more recent sighting.'

'Oh yes. I met him in Marseille in the 1990s and he's as mad as a biscuit!' This *was* a story I could tell them and I did so with great enthusiasm, leaving out only the part about him making Nanette and her staking him.

Serge had been quite deranged. He had wanted to recreate his murdered family and was searching for people that resembled them to turn into vampires. He'd started with Nanette who reminded him of his wife, but she had staked him when he started to stalk a child. According to Nanette, she'd done it because she didn't want to babysit a vampire child for ever more, but I thought maybe it had been because she was a new vampire and still had some morality and human feeling left in her.

'Is Serge still in Marseille?' Pierre asked.

'He could be. We haven't remained in touch. As I said, he was a few sandwiches short of a picnic, but if you want I could maybe help you pick up his trail again.'

'How would we know if a vampire was active in an area? What would we need to look for?' asked Jean-Claude looking at me intently through the glass. He was gauging whether I was telling the truth. *Get me the internet and I'll find you one!* Problem was that would probably expose Carl-Heinz and Nanette too.

'Well, I always preyed on the less fortunate in society, so you might find the body of a tramp in a river with all his blood drained from him. Look for bodies of dogs, again drained of blood.' That was my MO in 1926. It might throw up a young and careless vampire somewhere. 'Or you could always place an online advert saying that you want a vampire to drink your blood. I met a very obliging German chap that way once,' I said smiling at the memory of Klaus. The two agents exchanged glances with each other before giving me a sceptical look. 'I'm telling you! Humans are bizarre at times! This guy let me cut his arm and drink his blood, problem was that he had a fondness for beer and bratwurst and it made him taste peculiar.'

'Any others we need to know about?' Pierre ploughed straight on, not letting me elaborate on the link between diet and blood flavour.

I sat back and thought for a moment, it annoyed me that they had so little interest in me the vampire, and in my experiences. They only wanted to solve crimes and trace other vampires. I too wanted to know if there were others out there. For one, I wanted to find Otto, my clever brother – we were of the same bloodline after all – but I wanted to trace him on my own. 'Sorry. Those are the only ones I know about. We tend to be solitary hunters and quite clever in covering our tracks,' I said, raising my hands in apology.

'We had a look at your computers and found a lot of chatrooms in your browsing history,' said Pierre.

'Those chatrooms are a hoot! There are all sorts of nutters there pretending to be vampires,' I said airily.

'But *you* were on there too,' said Jean-Claude looking at me rather smugly.

'Well you *might* find a vampire on there, but trust me, most chatters are 14-year-old girls that read too much,' I said calmly. I had not wanted them to explore the internet; hopefully my two friends would be careful and keep their digital heads down.

'So who is Nanette?'

Fuck! This is getting uncomfortable! I realised I had opened a whole new can of worms by trying to make friends. I should've kept my mouth shut, behaved as well as I could and just taken their mistrust and dislike on the chin. I'm impulsive and often do things without thinking it through. I had to be on my guard with these agents otherwise they would be sniffing in areas I did not want them rooting around in. I composed myself and went on, looking as unperturbed as I could.

'I met her at a fancy dress party once. That girl has a serious vampire fetish, but she is very human I can assure you,' I answered. 'I cottoned on that she was Queen of Fangs.'

'You asked her to come to Paris when you went on the run. Why?' asked Pierre.

'I thought she might help me, but she never turned up,' I said shrugging my shoulders.

'We would like to question this Nanette.'

'Contact her via the chatroom, that's how I got in touch with her,' I said nonchalantly.

'We're trying that, but she is not responding. You don't have a last name or mobile number?' asked Pierre.

They were calm, but I sensed keen interest and felt they knew I was being evasive.

'Can you not trace the IP address?' I asked.

The two agents looked at each other. I got the distinct impression that it was them being evasive now.

'You also talked to a Dutch man about tracing a German vampire,' said Pierre.

Fuck! OK, this is getting really uncomfortable now!

'Yeah. I yanked his chain good and proper. I'm on the internet a lot and came across the same stuff he had, so I just spun him along. You both know I get bored easily. I wanted to distract the guy from chasing me! He was actually on to me in Cannes. I can give you his real name,' I said smiling.

'We have that, thanks Cameron. We are emailing him with some questions,' said Pierre.

'Be careful. Before you know it stories will be doing the rounds online that the French secret service has a vampire in custody,' I said jokingly. I could see they were very unsatisfied with the morning's session. I hadn't given them anything more than they already knew and they clearly suspected I was holding out. I was led back to my cell and left there for two days.

***

The dog they had given me was a good-natured golden retriever cross that liked to play and didn't get too upset about the biting. I decided to call the bitch Blondie. I don't normally go about naming my food, but I felt that Blondie and I were going to get along and that we were forming a closer bond than was usual in the vampire-food relationship. I was so jealous when it got taken for walks outside. I would love to have taken it myself and gone for a good run in the park – I was going seriously stir crazy locked up alone and needed to smell the outside air. Eventually, I couldn't take it any more and I banged on the door until I got to speak to an agent. Pierre came alone as Jean-Claude was on leave for a few days.

'I need to go outside, get a bit of exercise. I'm doing my best to stay calm, but I need this,' I pleaded.

Pierre was silent for a moment, before saying, 'Unfortunately, Cameron, we feel that you have not been co-operating fully with us.'

Damn! They were blackmailing me! I felt driven into a corner, one that I couldn't bullshit my way out of. I feared things would get much worse if I didn't give them something and I paced around my cell quickly trying to calculate what I was willing to give them in return for much-needed exercise. 'OK. I'll give you the name of the German vampire if you let me go outside and do some exercise,' I said, a little desperately.

Pierre had to go and deliberate with his boss and both of them came back to talk to me. As the headquarters were in

42

such a built-up area they couldn't let me run around the neighbourhood, but they did agree to let me up on to the roof for an hour each night, and to let me use their gym for an hour a day. It was better than nothing and would help to relax me a little.

That first night, it felt fantastic being out in the night air and breathing in the smells of all the different humans and animals in the vicinity. I hadn't known how badly I needed space until I was locked up for days on end. It made me nervous and stopped me from thinking clearly, so I'd been trapped and coerced into divulging information I didn't want them to have. I had been delusional thinking that they would be in awe of this mighty vampire and thankful that I was on their side. I took in a few lungfuls of fresh air and decided to make the best of a bad situation. The guards were wary of me at first, but I can be very charming and my cheerful banter is usually infectious. While it felt good to interact with others and be outside, I couldn't imagine lasting long in this place – I was one big scary accident waiting to happen.

Chapter 6: Joseph

The morning after my first rooftop visit, they came to get me early and let me exercise for an hour in the gym – *very wise to try to tire me out before the interview!* I was escorted to the interview room at about ten o'clock where I saw that Jean-Claude had returned.

'Good break?' I asked him jovially. 'Go anywhere nice?'

'Family visit,' he answered brusquely, unwilling to tell me more. 'So. The name of the German?' he asked, coming straight to the point.

I wasn't going to let him off the hook that easily, though. He should have known by now that being evasive only made me more curious and unlikely to co-operate until I had something.

'Family visit? Hmm. I do hope all your relatives are well. Do you still have your parents?'

He sighed and grudgingly told me, 'It was a wedding. A cousin got hitched. The bride looked lovely and a good time was had by all. Can we get on now?'

'What was for dinner?' I continued, feigning interest just to be annoying.

'There was a choice of salmon or chicken.' He was working hard not to get riled.

'And the starter and pudding?'

Even behind the thick glass I could sense his blood pressure beginning to rise. I really should have told him to get it checked, but killing this man without even having to get my fangs out would be way more fun.

From between gritted teeth he answered, 'There was a choice between a goats cheese tart and duck to start. The dessert was a crème brûlée.'

'Crème brûlée. Bit unimaginative,' I said disapprovingly.

'It was a very nice crème brûlée and now that you are intimately familiar with the menu, could you acquaint me with the name of the German vampire?'

Getting bored with my own game, I obliged.

'Carl-Heinz Heller, born in Berlin in 1875. You probably won't believe me, but in Berlin there was a professor that had managed to catch a female vampire. He invited his brightest student over to his house and had the vampire kill him and bring him back to life with her own blood. The professor had developed a drug that made vampires obedient, you see.'

The two agents straightened up in their seats at the mention of the drug.

'Is this drug still available?' asked Pierre.

'The professor is long since dead and the drug was not found to be that effective. According to Carl-Heinz it worked only on him and then only for about 50 years.

'Fifty years isn't bad. Where is the drug now?' asked Pierre.

'Lost somewhere in the mists of World War Two.'

I wasn't keen to be rushed through my story or to be speculating about the stupid drug, so I took them back to the beginning and told them the entire story of Professor Lindtman and his more ambitious cousin who'd tried to make money by selling the whole experiment to the military. I told them about all the terrible side effects of the drugs and the military's use of Carl-Heinz and how he had made me.

'Carl-Heinz really is the only one the drug worked on,' I told them, but I could feel their reluctance to believe me and knew that they would love to get their mittens on the drug anyway.

'So he was your maker?' asked Pierre.

'Yes. I wasn't keen to surrender my maker to you. I hope you understand,' I explained.

They wanted to know where he was now and I told them the rest of Carl-Heinz's story: how the Nazis had used him, how he'd fallen into Soviet hands and how he'd finally managed to escape and regain his long lost freedom. I referred them to my email conversations with the Dutch vampire historian who had found some stories about Carl-Heinz online, including his flight over the Berlin wall in 1973. I finished with the fact that I had met him in Berlin.

'I'm not sure if he's still there, he was talking to me about going to Rome as he had an interest in archaeology,' I said, leaving out the fact that he would probably never have plucked up the courage to leave Berlin. I didn't tell them that he liked to feed in hospitals either, hoping that even with all this information it would still be pretty impossible to find him. Frankly most of this information was already out there and I couldn't do much to protect Carl-Heinz. I was sure the German authorities would think the French had lost the plot if they came to them with a story about a vampire living in Berlin.

They seemed to be happy with the morning session so we broke for lunch. The dog snoozed with her head on my lap while I looked through the papers: they'd given me a good selection of English language and French titles. I liked reading papers. Well, I liked reading the front page then turning over to the sports and the comics. My favourite was reading the obituaries – having been on the Riviera party scene for a number of years, I had to come to know a lot of rich, old and important people. Their obituaries ended up in the national papers and I loved reading the wonderful things that were said about often not-so-wonderful people.

My eye fell on an obituary in the *New York Times*. Joseph Franklin Webber 1927-2012, it read. In the 1920s I had lived in Paris and was sharing an apartment with my artist girlfriend Hélène. It was through her that I'd met many interesting and wealthy people, including Joseph's father Charley Webber. He was a fabulously wealthy American who had chosen to live in Paris to get away from his overbearing parents. He was a great guy and we had become firm friends. When the stock market crashed in 1930, his family lost a large part of their fortune and he'd had to leave Paris and return to America. It made my head hurt to think that I had known this 85-year-old, recently-deceased man as a baby. I read the whole obituary. It talked in glowing terms about Joseph's contribution to the American economy, but also about his charity work and deep Christian faith. I smiled again at the difference between father and son. Charley had been a hedonistic booze-hound with a healthy disrespect for religion.

I lay back on the bed thinking about Charley and the Paris of the 1920s. It had been a wonderful time and I still wished I could have gone back and done things differently. I had lived for a very long time and made many mistakes, but I still didn't feel old and wise; the years hadn't robbed me entirely of my lust for life or made me feel much different than when I was actually 20. I felt just as young and restless now, and ached to go out and do what 20-year-olds liked to do. I missed female company and was dying to go and chase lassies again. On top of that I had acquired a lust for hunting: stalking prey and feeding on humans. Being locked up made me very dangerous and though I was aware of it, I could do nothing to change it.

***

In the afternoon, they wanted to know more about Carl-Heinz and even brought in a sketch artist to get a likeness. I wanted him to do a portrait of me, as I hadn't seen myself for 98 years, but my pleas fell on deaf ears. In retaliation, I gave them a bullshit description of Carl-Heinz which, in spite of the true details of him being tall and blond, led the artist to sketch something more like Dolph Lundgren. We called it a day at about five o'clock, and I was led back to my cell.

I tried to make the best of the evening by playing with the dog and reading some comic books. I was taken up to the roof at about 11 o'clock where I paced around restlessly. I estimated the building to be about five or six storeys high and noted that to the side there were some trees that could break a fall. I was pretty indestructible and I believed I could escape from this roof. I knew where the nearest metro station was, having done my research before I handed myself in. I did some exercises and jogged around for the remainder of the hour, watched closely by my two armed guards.

The exercise did calm me down a little. I had thought that drinking Jean-Claude's blood a few days before would have seen me alright for a little longer, but it hadn't. I just wanted more.

Chapter 7: Monique

I had decided to ration the dog and just have small breakfasts. I got on well with this mutt and wanted her to last. Being on a diet didn't help my edginess, but Christ knew how much time they would take to find me another food supply. When I was next led to the interview room however, I caught a whiff of something different. I could smell Jean-Claude with his slightly too high blood pressure but I also could smell healthy blood with a faster heart rate. Women have faster heart rates than men and I was sure that there was one on the other side of the glass. When the light went on, I saw I was right. There she was, brown hair swept tightly back in a sensible ponytail and glasses that gave her an even sterner look. I guessed she was in her late thirties. *I bet you're a panther in the bedroom once you let your hair down!* I fantasised lustfully as Jean-Claude introduced her as Monique Fabian, psychiatrist. Then he left us alone, on our separate sides of the glass, after showing her demonstratively where the panic button was. He really left out no opportunity to point out that I was a dangerous animal, and not to be trusted.

'Good morning, Monsieur Blair. I would like to ask you some questions, if I may?' she asked.

'You may, *if* you call me Cameron,' I said with my most charming smile, imagination running rampant. *I could turn her; we could cause murder and mayhem in the facility and flee together into the night!*

She explained that she had been called in as there was some concern about my mental state and therefore, by extension, about the safety of the agents working at headquarters.

'I'm sure I'm perfectly normal for a vampire,' I said, slightly miffed. 'We're only having the occasional mishap because people just aren't listening to me. They want me to be human and I'm not.'

'That's exactly why I'm here: to listen to you and to understand you,' she said, smiling. 'I hope that with my help and input we can all work better together.'

'It really is quite simple, Monique. If they fed me better and gave me access to the internet, I'd be much calmer and more co-operative,' I said, not sure what she was likely to achieve.

'Would you die if you didn't drink blood?' she asked.

I was surprised that no one had posed that question before, but I was uneasy that it was a psychiatrist who had. *No! I need more food, not less!*

'I most certainly would and it's an agonising way to go!' I said, vehemently.

I told her how I had once witnessed a vampire starve himself. The stomach pain had become unbearable, then he'd started to lose strength before slipping slowly into a delirious, semi-conscious state. I had stepped in at that point and force-fed the vampire some cow's blood. This had been George's father and he had never forgiven me for bringing him back a second time. I also told her about an experiment Carl-Heinz had witnessed in his facility. They had starved one of the vampires and kept him firmly locked in his cell. Carl-Heinz had heard him scream as the pain started to send the poor creature insane. On the seventh night, the screams suddenly stopped; the vampire had broken his chair and used the wooden splinters to stake himself through the heart.

'You see, Monique, some fates really are worse than death. Please don't make me go hungry.'

'There are some things we can't give you, such as the internet, but I'm here to help you and see if there are other

50

ways we can make you more at ease. You are a talking, thinking rational being and we think we can help you more, apart from just feeding you,' she said with a sympathetic smile.

That sounded promising. Then she suggested we start with a standard IQ test.

'I won't do very well at that. I was rubbish at school!' I said, my good humour fast disappearing.

'You won't be judged,' she said taking a note 'we just have no record of a vampire's intelligence.'

'We're not all the same,' I said, crossing my arms defensively, leaning back and staring back at her.

'I'll tell you what. We'll start with something else.' She disappeared from view and I heard her rummage around for something. She pulled out some cards with what looked like inkblots on them.

'It's a little old fashioned and not all psychiatrists believe in the usefulness of this exercise, but I would love to hear your responses to these,' she said enthusiastically. 'I think I'll just put the rule books aside and try some different things. You are a vampire after all.'

I recognised the cards. I'd read about the Rorschach test and was equally keen to have a go. My wild imagination would probably have her typing up scientific publications for the next decade. I had a lot of fun describing the inkblots and I got her to smile a couple of times, then she told me she was going to say random words and I should respond with the first thing that came into my head.

'If you are looking to diagnose me, I could spare you the trouble. My friend George classed me as a psychopath.'

'Is this George a qualified psychiatrist?' she asked, surprised.

'No, but he is mostly right about me. We've known each other for a long time.'

'I'd like to do the word association anyway, so I can get to know you a bit better too. Shall we start?'

'Ok,' I said hesitantly. I'm very impulsive, so I was dreading this. I knew I had to be a little on my guard otherwise she might be on to something that would get under my skin.

'Just relax Cameron, I'm not here to trip you up.'

She gave me such a nice smile that I almost believed her. She did have a gorgeous smile that showed off a row of even white teeth.

'Mother,' she started.

'Home,' I said

'Father.'

'Work,' I said, as my dad and I used to work together at the brewery.

'Death.'

I saw her flick a look at me, waiting for my response.

'War,' I said quickly.

'Blood.'

'Happiness.' I could see her scribbling away at this response. It was true, but I wasn't sure what she was going to make of it, and before I could change my answer the next word came.

'Discipline.'

'School.'

'Patience?' she asked

'None.' She looked up at me, questioningly.

'Er, chess?' I revised, eventually.

'Art.'

Hélène was on the tip of my tongue but I managed to stop

52

and said Picasso instead. I relaxed a little after that as I felt I had some control over the test, but I suppose she might have read something else into it altogether. We went on for a while longer and I was more at ease enjoying the company of an intelligent woman. She wouldn't tell me her diagnosis though.

'You're very artistic, aren't you Cameron?' was all she said at the end of the test.

'No, I just learned a lot from a talented artist.'

She looked at me as though she wanted me to continue. I wasn't ready to go there yet so I continued airily, 'I knew Matisse and Picasso when I lived in Paris in the 1920s. A lot of artists worked and lived there at that time, so I learned a lot and I learned from the best.'

'Do you paint yourself?' she asked.

'Never thought of it. I don't think I could improve on the greats.' In all my years of appreciating art I had never felt the temptation to pick up a brush. I was surprised I hadn't thought of it before.

'I think you should try. You might derive a lot of pleasure from it,' she said encouragingly. 'I'll see if we can get you some artist's materials.'

Wow, she's good! In a morning she's found something that might tame the beast. 'I'll give it a try. Thank you.'

'You're welcome. And bring me your work for our next session,' she said, packing her things away. 'And you know art, Cameron, it doesn't have to be pretty or realistic, just express yourself.'

I was rather excited when I got back to my cell. I *should* create! I had knowledge and taste and lots of spare time... I decided to start straight away and doodled away for a few hours on the *Financial Times*, trying to capture Blondie's likeness.

53

***

In the afternoon, it was back to business. They wanted to know more about the murders I had committed and I was pleased they wanted to talk about something other than vampires I might know. I sat back and waxed lyrical about the late eighties and early nineties, which had been a prosperous time for me. I had nurtured and established a network of criminal contacts around the Riviera stretching to Monaco and Italy. I was wealthy and dressed like all the other rich young things coming to the Côte d'Azur to play and spend their parents' money. People came and went so I had a good social life without having to get close to anyone. Apart from the occasional old biddy that died of natural causes (perhaps helped along ever so slightly if she found me in her apartment) I didn't cause any other deaths. I decided not to tell the agents about these.

In 1984, I sold my apartment in the Avenue Gambetta and got a much more expensive place overlooking the port of Nice. I had become fascinated with yachts and loved hanging around with people who could afford them.

'How do you buy and sell flats when you can't go out during the day,' piped up Pierre.

'That was becoming more difficult. I needed bank accounts once you couldn't do all your transactions with cash any more. I often hired someone I trusted to impersonate me and go in with false paperwork to set up an account and deal with things. Also, estate agents are willing to show flats and do paperwork late at night if there are large sums of money involved. To be honest Pierre, if you have money, most things are possible,' I explained.

'Didn't the banks or inland revenue ever question your

earnings?' Pierre asked me, amazed.

'I had a lot of time on my hands during the day, so I set up a confusing paper trail of me being a business consultant, and there was a lot of back and forth of receipts between me and my criminal contacts. I did declare taxes etc, but every ten years or so I faked my own death and started up again under a new name.'

'Were you ever investigated?' Pierre asked.

'Never. Ten years seems to be the time frame before any alarm bells go off. I had a nice corrupt notary at the time that legally passed my estate on to my "nephew" who was basically me with my new identity,' I told him.

As computers and technology took over, things got easier but also more complicated. I embraced the new technology and got it to work to my advantage. I made a lot of money on gambling sites when they started to emerge. Finally! Some legal income! But me being me, I wanted more and I didn't want to give up the burglaries. This led me to tell them about another murder I'd committed in the nineties. I had read about a local silversmith who had created a fabulous chalice and other items for a church.

'I thought you couldn't handle silver?' Pierre interrupted.

'Nothing a pair of gloves can't solve,' I said 'and I really wanted to have a closer look at these items as photos don't do such things justice.'

I'd broken into the church and entered hesitantly, half expecting a bolt of lightning or something, but all remained calm. When I couldn't find anything in the church itself, I'd looked in the rectory. I searched all the rooms thoroughly and discovered a small safe. It was archaic and looked to be no challenge for someone with my skill set, but without warning the lights had come on and a man in pyjamas was standing right behind me. When I'm startled, my fangs spring out and instinct takes over, so before I knew it I had my fangs planted in his neck.

'You killed a priest?' asked Jean-Claude and both agents looked at me aghast.

'I know, it's meant to bring seven years bad luck,' I said sitting back and scratching my head. I had blamed every scrap of misfortune that had befallen me since 1992 on this murder, but in truth there hadn't been that much in the seven years that followed.

'I never heard that killing priests brings seven years of bad luck,' said Pierre bemused. 'Isn't it breaking a mirror that's meant to do that?'

'I don't know. I always get these old wives' tales mixed up. Mirrors, priests and black cats, they all freak me out,' I said shuddering involuntarily.

'So what did you do with the priest?' asked Jean-Claude.

'I lifted one of the flagstones in the church and buried him underneath. He was more or less my size so I packed a bag with some clothes I liked. He had decent taste for a priest and I thought a shirt with a dog collar might come in handy. I tidied the place up and made it look like the priest had just decided to leave locking the door behind him.'

'That is terrible, making it look like this honourable man had run off with the church silver!' cried Jean-Claude.

'The besmirching of his good name seems to upset you more than his murder!' I had struck a nerve with Jean-Claude and was pleased to have found a weakness in this obviously religious man.

'Can you tell us the name of this church?' asked Jean-Claude composing himself. 'We might at least clear his name yet.'

I told them the name and location of the church and we stopped the interview there. It was already six o'clock and the agents must've been keen to get back to their families. I realised I knew nothing about the two men who were beginning to know so much about me. I thought I might get them to talk about themselves the following day.

When I was led back to my cell, I discovered that they had indeed got me some sketchpads, pastels and pencils. With the dog curled up beside me, I sat cross-legged on the bed drawing for a few hours until they came to take me for my midnight stroll. Luc and Cyrille were on duty, so I just exercised. There was never any point in trying to draw them into conversation. I didn't mind – they were just doing their jobs – but if it came to escaping I would kill them without a moment's hesitation.

When I got back from the rooftop, I looked at my doodles. Hélène had been a wonderful draftswoman and my doodles looked childish in comparison. I had not managed to capture the likeness or proportions of the dog at all. For some reason, its head looked too small for its body. It had amused me and had made the time pass more quickly, but I realised I wasn't a natural talent. I booted up my laptop and decided to give art another try later.

Chapter 8: Siobhan

'I thought we might talk about you today,' I started off the interview. 'You know so much about me and I know nothing about you two.'

The two agents looked at each other before Jean-Claude answered, indulgently, 'It's not our usual practice to divulge personal information to a suspect. You have to understand that we wouldn't want personal information used against us.'

'Make up shit! That's what I do if I don't want to tell you something,' I encouraged, grinning. 'I'd just like a normal, two-way conversation for a change.'

Another look was exchanged between the two men, everything I'd ever told them now in question. *Oops. That probably wasn't the best thing to say!*

'I would advise you to take this more seriously, Cameron,' said Jean-Claude.

'Or what? You'll torture me even more than you already have?' I said throwing my arms up in the air in desperation. I was bored and frustrated and the interviews were getting tedious. I found the agents' accusations and moral judgements insulting: in my maybe not so humble opinion I had been a rather kind-hearted vampire. Compared with some of the vampires depicted in films, I was positively angelic!

'I think we're treating you better than you deserve. You have won a number of concessions, but we can easily take those away again!' said Jean-Claude drily.

I desperately wanted my painting back so I decided to not push them any further. Resigned, I asked what they wanted to know this time.

'You killed a priest in 1992. Today the police are searching the church after we gave them an anonymous tip-off. I'm sure we'll hear about it when they find a body.'

'Seems like a waste of police time. They'll have to investigate and do forensics without any hope of catching the killer,' I said.

'The family does like to know if a loved one is dead or alive,' explained Pierre.

I shrugged my shoulders. I couldn't care less.

'Who else have you murdered since 1992?' asked Jean-Claude. I gave him a long cold stare to show my displeasure at the loaded question.

There had been something in 1993, but I didn't really want to tell them about it – it was a bit embarrassing. After thinking for while, though, I decided I should. George had phoned me and told me he had taken two weeks leave from his army job. He had previously been stationed in Germany, but he was now back in England having joined the SAS. He told me he needed to see me urgently and though he didn't tell me why, I agreed immediately. We'd decided to meet in Calais, in a local bar in town, and as soon as I walked in I'd spotted George sitting at a table, head in hands and clearly upset. When I joined him at his table and asked him what was wrong, he couldn't look me in the eye, but gradually he revealed to me what had happened back in England.

George had a younger sister Olivia who was 19 at the time. I'd never had much interest in the girl as she seemed to be taking after her mother and father and was shy and serious. She had finished her A levels without much trouble and was now studying something clever at the London School of Economics. After some urging, George told me his sister had been raped when she was walking home alone after a night out with some friends.

'That *is* awful,' I said. 'Did she go to the police?'

'She did,' he said, his face like thunder. 'They told her there had been another two cases that month, but she got the impression it wasn't much of a priority for them. She told me that giving a statement to some middle-aged cops that obviously didn't care about her, but wanted to know every lurid detail, was almost as bad as the rape itself.'

I genuinely felt for George. I didn't have a sister, but I could imagine his anguish.

'Would you like me to help trace the bastard?' I asked. Moral justification was an added bonus to killing.

'I'll even turn a blind eye if we catch the pervert,' he answered grimly.

So George took me across the channel in the boot of his car. As usual, he'd been quite thorough in his research and had a lot of information about the other cases, including their locations. We proceeded to stake out both parks where the attacks had taken place, taking a park each and waiting in the shrubbery to see if any passers by matched the physical description Olivia had given George. She hadn't been able to give him much, but she was pretty sure he was taller than her at about six foot and he'd been wearing a camouflage jacket when he'd jumped out of the bushes to drag her back in. He had also worn a black balaclava, so we hadn't much else to go on, but what she'd said matched the descriptions the two other victims had given.

We spent a week hiding out hoping to get lucky and spot the guy until eventually George told me he had to report back to his barracks, as he had only managed to get a few weeks leave from his job with the SAS. 'Can you continue alone?' he'd asked.

'I think so. I'll gift wrap him if I find him,' I said, smiling.

'I'm not sure if I should thank you. You seem to be enjoying yourself a little too much,' he said, looking at me searchingly. 'I have seen a few missing dog posters going up in the area!'

'A man's got to eat! Stakeouts work up an appetite!'

George raised his eyebrows but didn't say any more. 'Do you need anything before I head off?' he asked.

George had rented us a flat for a few weeks so I was comfortable during the day. He'd been right though; I *was* rather enjoying myself. England was having a decent summer that year and hanging out in London when the nights were warm was no hardship for me.

'I might need some help getting back over the channel at some point,' I told him.

'Call me when you're done. I'll sort something out.'

We parted company and I continued the vigil alone. It might take longer to catch the rapist with only one pair of eyes, but having little else to do I did enjoy the occasional dog that wandered into my hideout. Then, during the second week, I got lucky. A man fitting the description walked right by me and disappeared into some scrub a few meters away. I exited from the back of my bushes and circled round in a wide arc to approach his position. I could just make him out between the branches as I closed in and saw that he had his back to me. He was wearing a balaclava and standing very still. *Bingo!* I ploughed straight in, tore off his balaclava and planted my fangs into his neck. He didn't struggle for long. When he went limp I dropped him and disguised my fang marks with some stab wounds. I had procured some nice pink ribbon and I wrapped it tightly around the guy and tied a very fetching bow on his chest. I laid him out on a park bench and made a hasty exit.

'What was embarrassing about that?' interrupted Pierre.

'Oh no, *that* murder was fine. And it happened in London anyway. I just thought I'd tell you the whole story from start to finish,' I explained impatiently. *You have to put a story in its proper context.*

'Continue, Cameron,' said Pierre.

The murder made the local paper immediately, but it made national news after an anonymous tip-off to the police had said that the murdered man was a serial rapist, responsible for at least three attacks in the area. DNA confirmed he was indeed the man suspected of multiple attacks.

'Vigilante Kills Sex Beast!' screamed the *Daily Mail*. 'Vigilante Leaves Police a Present' quipped the *Daily Mirror*. The papers had loved the bow and published every graphic detail they could get hold of about the attacks. George had an airtight alibi, so after a few days I gave him a call.

'You did say you would gift-wrap him,' the voice came drily from the other end.

'Olivia must be in hell, but it may help that this guy is gone,' I told him quietly.

'Thanks, Cameron.'

'Pleasure was all mine, George. Now, can you get me back to Calais?'

'A mate owes me a huge favour. I'll get him to give you a lift back,' he informed me.

'One of your mates from the old days?' I asked.

'Yeah, but you can trust him. He'll do what I tell him and not bother you with any questions.'

George's friend was a skinhead with a white van on his way to Calais to pick up cheap booze and bring it back to the UK. He hid me under some blankets in the back of the van and never asked me a single question. I got back to my car in Calais without any problems. My contact in Italy, Paolo, had got me a sleek black Audi Quattro that was a joy to drive fast. It was stolen, but he'd put new number plates on it. Paolo traded in all sorts of things and usually got me a very nice German motor with a spacious boot if I needed to go anywhere.

'Do you know how many cylinders an Audi Quattro has?' I asked the agents.

Jean-Claude gave me a quizzical look but Pierre smiled and answered, 'Five. My Dad used to have one. He had a thing for German cars too.'

Jean-Claude shot his colleague a quick disapproving look and Pierre rapidly asked me to continue.

'Anyway. This is where things went a bit haywire,' I continued.

'What happened?' asked Pierre.

'It had just got dark when I started my drive south and just a few kilometres down the road I saw a girl holding a sign for Nice.'

'A hitch-hiker?' asked Jean-Claude.

'I hadn't had a decent conversation for a while and thought maybe she'd be attracted to me and be up for some awkward sex in the back of the car.'

Jean-Claude glared at me with utter contempt. 'What happened?' he asked, reluctantly. The last thing he wanted to hear about was me shagging a hitch-hiker. 'Is she dead?'

'Hold your horses! I'll tell you what happened all in good time!' I've always liked telling stories, embellishing or leaving out details to enhance narrative and I wasn't going to be rushed on this one.

'Continue,' sighed Pierre, equally unenthusiastically.

'I had to give the girl a lift. It was dark and there could've been all sorts of dangerous men out there,' I continued with a big grin. 'After what had happened to Olivia, I felt it was my duty to protect the poor girl and not leave her out there alone in the dark.'

Jean-Claude's eyes narrowed in anger, but he kept quiet.

'She was Irish and had just come off the boat too. Her first lift hadn't taken her very far, but the driver had assured her that it was a good spot to get picked up by people travelling south. "You're in luck," I told her and she got in.'

I carried on. She was small and must have been about 18 or 19, but she had a nice smile in a face covered with freckles. She had thick, curly, red hair which she'd tied up with a green scrunchy. I hadn't been quite sure what to do with her once she was in the car. I couldn't take her to a hotel room as she would want to continue the journey with me and wouldn't understand why I only drove at night and wanted to stay in a dark room for 16 hours. Siobhan, as she was called, was a very bubbly wee girl and she'd chatted away non-stop, telling me about her five brothers back in Ireland and where she was planning to go on her travels. She'd taken her shoes off and planted her dirty, bare feet on the dashboard. The car was nicked, but I still hadn't liked having filthy footprints all over the dashboard. She'd also lit a cigarette and just flicked the ash carelessly towards the ashtray, most of it missing its target. I'd found myself thinking I could just kill her. There were no witnesses, I was hungry and I'd quickly deduced that she wouldn't be the type to have sex in the back of the car with a complete stranger. I'd decided to drive on for a few hours, then stop at a quiet rest stop and have her for dinner.

'Did you rape her?' asked Jean-Claude.

'How dare you! I don't *rape* women! I *love* women!' I shouted, outraged. 'Have you not been listening to a word I've been saying for the last few hours?'

'You do kill them, though, so where exactly does the line lie with you?' asked Jean-Claude.

The moralistic, sanctimonious bastard! My hatred for the man deepened; not torturing my food was usually one of my rules, but for him I would gladly make an exception. 'I'm sure you've killed people, being in the secret service and all,' I cried, 'but I don't for a minute think you'd ever rape someone!'

'So killing is fine, but rape isn't?'

'Exactly! As my maker Carl-Heinz said "One shouldn't torture the poor unfortunate food".'

Jean-Claude scowled at me again, then gestured for me to continue.

'We stopped when she needed the loo. I got out to stretch my legs and wandered away from the Audi. Suddenly I heard my car starting, the headlights came on and the car came towards me at great speed. All I could do was jump out of the way and watch as the red backlights disappeared into the distance. I felt like a complete fool! All I'd had to do was take the keys out of the ignition and she would have been dinner!'

'A lucky escape for Miss Ireland there!' said Pierre grinning.

'I wouldn't say that. I had some of my nicest Armani pieces in the boot. I was going to hunt this little bitch down,' I said. Even now I was still fuming about the whole incident. The smile had disappeared off Pierre's face. He was a romantic at heart and must've hoped for a happy ending. 'Anyway, we'll get to that later,' I continued. 'First I had the problem of being stuck at a rest stop without a car.'

It was two o'clock in the morning, so there were a few hours of darkness left yet. The traffic was light with just the occasional lorry thundering by, so I hid in some scrub for a few hours, hoping an unsuspecting motorist would stop. By four o'clock I knew I had to find a hiding place for the day. A few hundred meters away, I found a derelict cowshed and built myself a safe place with some branches and an old bathtub that had been used as a watering trough for the animals.

As it was summer, it was a very long and boring day. When the sun finally disappeared behind the horizon and I was able to get out I was filthy and dishevelled and no one in their right mind would have stopped to give me a lift. I had to lie in wait and hope a lone motorist would eventually show up. Then, at about 11 o'clock that night a big lorry pulled up and a fat, hairy man in a string vest got out and headed for the toilets. I waited for him to come out and jumped on the unsuspecting driver with great enthusiasm; I was hungry and I'd never driven such a large truck before – that would be exciting! I hid the corpse a few hundred meters away in a ditch and covered it with stones and earth. By the time I was done, I was covered in muck so I tried to clean up as best as I could at the small sink in the toilets. Then I got into the lorry and had a look around. It was a big rig and behind the seats was a cabin with bedding where I could hide during the day. The many gears looked complicated but I had driven all sorts of vehicles since the 1920s so I was confident I would get to grips with this beast soon enough.

I got out again and had a look at what it contained. The truck had Belgian number plates and I was very pleased to find that it contained beer; that would be worth quite a few bob and be easy to sell so I stood to make a nice profit into the bargain. I started up the engine and set off slowly. After some jumps and shudders I got the rig up to speed and joined the quiet motorway traffic.

'Could you give us the location of the rest stop?' asked Pierre

'Get me a map and I'll mark the location of the body,' I offered. A road map of France was found and I marked the location. As it had been such an embarrassing incident, the exact spot had been forever engraved in my memory.

I drove on until I reached a rest stop that was livelier and had a restaurant, a bar with a phone and – more interestingly – some girls that were happy to entertain passing truck-drivers. I called my contact Paolo and told him what had fallen into my hands. He sounded very interested and assured me he would mobilise some people to shift both the beer and the truck. Everything would be ready for my arrival the next night.

'Could you give us Paolo's details?' asked Pierre.

'I'd love to, but he died a few years ago. Most of his crew have moved on and I wouldn't know what they were doing now,' I said, sounding apologetic. It was a lie and they probably knew it. Paolo had been an excellent contact over the years and I wasn't keen to throw him under the bus.

'Very convenient,' said Jean-Claude sarcastically.

'It was a very nasty car crash. I lost a good friend that day,' I said pulling a glum face, doing my best to make Jean-Claude feel guilty.

'I'm sure you cried for days.'

'Anyway... around midnight I decided to have some fun and continue the drive after some of my other urges were dealt with.'

I could see the two agents looking uncomfortable again so I launched into my story with relish. Geneviève had been pleasantly surprised when such a young, attractive boy had invited her into his truck. Her usual clients were older, usually overweight and much sweatier.

'You don't even seem old enough to have a driving licence,' she had said smiling.

'Trust me, I'm older than I look,' I said, crawling into the cabin behind the seats. I unzipped my trousers and she got down to business. She was very good at her job and it didn't take me long to climax. I paid her and she left. I got behind the wheel and drove on for another few hours until I had to stop for daylight. The driver had a couple of good crime novels in his cabin and a nice porn mag, so the day passed quickly enough.

The two agents looked bored and said they wanted to pause for lunch. They really hated it when I talked about sex and girls, so I liked to give them graphic details to make them squirm, especially when it was entirely irrelevant to the murder in question.

'Where did you take the lorry?' Pierre asked me after the break.

'Scrapyard between Ventimiglia and San Remo, just over the French-Italian border.' There might be a scrapyard between Ventimiglia and San Remo, but it wouldn't be Paolo's.

'What happened to it?' asked Pierre. I didn't think they would do anything with this information, but was sure they knew I was feeding them bull crap.

'It was broken up for parts and the beer was loaded into smaller vehicles that evening and sold on to some local bars and restaurants.' That was true, but it had been in the Toulon area, not Italy.

'And the Irish girl?' Pierre enquired.

'I asked Paolo's crew to have a look out for her. A little, red-haired Irish girl in a big Audi Quattro wouldn't be too hard to find if she'd gone to Nice,' I said grimly.

'You found her?' Pierre asked again.

'I phoned around all my contacts giving them her description, and after a few days one of them spotted her in Antibes. According to my source, she was working in a bar in the town.'

'Was it her?' the younger agent asked.

'I decided to check it out and headed for Antibes. I did find a small redhead working in a pub, but she was English and not the girl I was after. I phoned all my contacts to update them about this girl and keep them looking.'

'And?' asked Pierre keen to get to point and the fate of the girl.

'It was another few days before I got another call and a tip about an English-speaking girl living in Nice. It sounded promising, as a black Audi had been spotted in the same street.'

I'd decided to stake the address out and see if it was her, and one night I spotted a redhead coming out of an apartment. It was indeed Siobhan. She got into the Audi and drove off, so I followed her in the BMW that Paolo had given me, along with some cash, in exchange for the lorry. Siobhan drove to the airport, parked up and went into the terminal. I waited until eventually she came back with a young man, a ginger like her. I got the impression it must be one of her brothers, as they looked so alike. This was bad news. Now there was someone there that knew her and would go to the police if she went missing.

'Why did you have to kill her?' interrupted Pierre.

'I never let anyone pull the wool over my eyes. If you piss me off, there will be consequences! I think it's a vampire thing. We can be *very* vindictive!' I said menacingly. The two agents glanced uneasily at each other and then told me to continue.

I stalked the two siblings for a few days and couldn't see a way to get near Siobhan without running into trouble. I could have broken into the flat and killed both of them, but I do hate giving the police too much to do. When I began to get bored of the whole thing I started to warm to the break-in option though, but before I could do it, they drove off together one night, heading towards the motorway and Italy. I followed them discreetly, waiting for a moment when we were the only traffic on the road.

Finally, I saw my opportunity. I sped up and clipped the left side of their car. The Audi spun out of control at high speed. In my rear view mirror I watched it turn on its side, flip up and go over the side railing.

'Did it kill them both?' asked Pierre looking shocked, but evidently still holding on to that glimmer of hope for a good ending.

'Don't know and don't care, but that part of the coast has some impressive drops down to the sea, so I think probably yes.'

'You didn't even get a meal out of it or any financial gain,' said Pierre and I could see he was getting upset, 'so why did you have to kill her?'

'I would have preferred a meal too, but I was getting bored of following her and this put an end to the whole thing.' Both men looked grim and said they wanted to stop for the day. I shrugged my shoulders and looked at my watch: it was only four o'clock.

A few hours after they'd led me back to the cell, Pierre came in with an armed guard. It was the first time in a while he'd been in the same room as me.

'You did kill both of them,' he said standing in the

doorway, looking coldly at me.

'And?' I asked nonchalantly, continuing my sketch of the dog.

'They were Siobhan and Dermot O'Connell from Limerick.'

'So?'

'Do you not care at all that you killed two innocent young people for no reason?'

'One innocent person! And you never know, he might've been a criminal too!' I said holding out my pencil and observing the dog for scale. Pierre watched me for a while then shook his head and walked out. I don't know what he'd expected. I'm not human! I don't do remorse and the bitch had nicked my car.

Chapter 9: Jean-Baptiste

I was asked, the following morning, to gather my drawings before I was led to the interview room. I was excited, as it meant Monique the psychiatrist would be there and I looked forward to seeing someone that treated me as a human being again. So far, we'd just chatted and done fun tests, but I knew full well she had been studying me and I was interested in finding out what she made of me. The guard took the drawings from me and locked me in the room. The light in the adjoining room came on and I could see her on the other side of the glass.

'Good morning, Cameron!'

'Good morning, Monique. How are you?'

'Very well. How have you been?'

'I'm much better now you are here,' I replied, smiling broadly.

'You've been busy, I see,' she said, smiling too while studying my doodles.

'They're not very good, but I've enjoyed making them.'

'Good! I see you have only drawn the dog. Did you not want to draw other things?' she asked.

'He's the only interesting thing in my cell,' I said gloomily.

'Don't you want to draw from memory? Things that have made you happy.'

'So you can analyse them?' I asked, mistrusting her motives.

'You don't trust humans?'

'No, I do. I just have my doubts about charming psychiatrists and the secret service,' I said, wryly.

'They took a painting from you. Can you tell me why that

upset you?' Monique continued.

'It was mine and I don't take kindly to people stealing my things. I told the agents yesterday what happened to the girl that nicked my car.' I crossed my arms and slumped moodily in my chair.

'How did you get the picture?'

I was getting annoyed by her harping on about the painting. 'Stole it, liked it, kept it,' I answered curtly.

'Why do you like it so much?'

'I have a suspicion it may be a Picasso. It could be worth a fortune,' I said glowering at her. *Enough already!*

'Is it the loss of the picture or the loss of money that annoys you the most?' she pushed on, oblivious to my irritation.

'It's the fact that they put their grubby mitts on my stuff that annoys me most!' I felt like throwing my chair against the glass, but that would only put the painting further out of reach. 'Can we talk about something else?' I asked, trying to control my anger.

'What would you like to talk about?'

'How about you? Have you got a husband and is he treating you well?' I asked.

She smiled, but didn't answer.

'Tell me what it feels like to bite someone?' she asked instead. 'When I said "blood" you replied "happiness".'

'OK. It's wonderful. The blood rushes though my body immediately. It's like really good sex, but without the exhaustion at the end; far from it – I'm full of energy afterwards and I feel happy.'

'What makes you stop?' she asked. 'Isn't the temptation to kill overwhelming?'

It was. At times it took all my willpower to take just a pint. I explained that we vampires knew above all not to get

73

noticed and to leave no clues behind. We had to control the bloodlust and ration our consumption of human blood. I often thought that drinking blood might be like taking drugs and human blood would be like cocaine: it made you feel fantastic but could lead to addiction and eventually to your undoing if you didn't control it strictly. Like any junky, procurement was all I could think of. I'd sell my granny for a bag of O positive right now.

'Hence the dog,' I said.

'Drinking dog blood stops you from wanting to attack humans?' she asked, but I could hear she didn't quite believe it. As with all humans, her opinions had been formed by films.

Animal blood, I imagined, was like smoking cigarettes: addictive, nice and it calmed and nourished me, but you wouldn't sell your granny for a packet of fags.

'It helps and I have actually grown to like dog a lot over the years.'

'What about sex? Do you need the blood to climax?' she asked.

Now we were on to a subject I did like! I relished the prospect of talking sex with my attractive psychiatrist, so I sat up in my chair and looked her in the eyes. I could see she wouldn't be easily shocked and wouldn't mind discussing fantasies.

'No, I enjoy sex for what it is, but blood does make it so much better. My fantasy would be a woman offering me her neck to bite.' I began to get slightly aroused just thinking about it.

'Has any woman ever let you bite her?'

'No. I've tried to do it, but it got me kicked out of bed and the poor girl freaked,' I recounted, smiling at the memory. 'Sensing the blood rushing under the skin is a very confusing and exciting experience but I find it best not to act on it. I often dose the girl with a sleeping pill.'

'You drug the girls?'

'Afterwards. The sex is always consensual, but the feeding isn't. I would like it to be, but so far I have only found one person who let me bite him.'

'You are bisexual?'

'I prefer women.' I gave her a wink. 'Especially clever brunettes! But when you've been a young man for as long as I have, there are few things you haven't tried!'

She smiled and actually blushed slightly. Then she wanted to talk about my life before I became a vampire and I happily spoke about my childhood in Edinburgh.

'How would you describe yourself before you became a vampire?' she asked.

'I was a normal bloke. I went to work and enjoyed being with my mates in my spare time. I was even engaged to be married.' I didn't mind talking about Fiona. It had been painful when I realised I would never see her again, but all our memories together had been sweet and innocent.

'And how do you see yourself now?' she asked after I talked for a while about my upbringing and early adulthood in Edinburgh.

'In many ways, I'm the same. This might sound strange to you but I still feel like I'm young and full of life. There is so much I want to see and do.' Then turning more serious I added, 'The blood has changed me though. It has robbed me of the qualities you humans consider to be virtues: honesty, not killing, et cetera.'

'So you are aware of your moral shortcomings. Don't you want to be a better man?'

'That boat has sailed, and frankly Monique, I don't care. I

only think about two things: blood and how not to get caught getting it.' Then I added quickly, 'Oh, and money too. So, three things.'

'For a man who says he has no morals, you are an interesting case. You did, after all, turn yourself in for a friend's benefit. I don't think you have completely lost your humanity.'

'I've lived a long time, Monique. I know I turned myself in, but I'm regretting it now. Don't think you have any hope of "curing" me – I'm getting worse every year. The best you lot can do here is keep me happy, which means giving me blood and not making me go on a diet because it seems, in your moralising eyes, the right thing to do. I know young Cameron is still in here, somewhere, but only if the vampire gets what he needs.'

She was scribbling away furiously and I felt rather defeated. I sensed she did have hopes of creating a reformed vampire, but it would be a pointless waste of her time trying. *What do I have to do to make them see that I am a nice guy, just not on an empty stomach?*

'Tell me more about your family.' She finally looked up from her notes.

Again, I was content to talk about my parents and brothers. I often looked back with fondness at my early years growing up with my two siblings and the neighbourhood kids. We didn't have much, but my friends and I didn't need the latest games to amuse ourselves; a dirty stream and some sticks did just fine. We didn't yet know what horrors were in store for us and how the Great War would change all our lives. We stopped when time was up and I'd just started talking about the army.

'We'll keep that for our next session as it's nearly

76

lunchtime. I do want you to continue with your art in the meantime. Do you want to draw me something other than the dog? I know you have your suspicions but I would like to see something personal,' she said.

'I'll see what comes out,' I said without much enthusiasm. I was hoping to start painting the dog. They'd given me a box of watercolours and I was itching to mess about with water and brushes and mix up some colours.

***

After a few hours back in my cell, the dynamic duo took over for the afternoon session.

'That's a very nice tie with a horrible shirt, Jean-Claude. Who bought you the tie?'

'Why do you assume someone else bought the tie?'

'Your outfits so far have been at best boring and at worst ghastly. Now, all of a sudden, there's this treasure around your neck!'

'I'm glad it pleases you,' Jean-Claude said sarcastically.

'Was it a present from your wife?' I pried further. He was hiding something.

'No,' Jean-Claude replied, looking uncomfortable. 'Can we get back to 1993 and the murders you committed after this date?'

'Aha! You have a mistress!' I declared triumphantly.

'No! It was an aunt that bought it!' he spluttered, his face turning even redder than it already was. 'Can we move on now?'

I knew he was lying and that I'd hit a nerve and I secretly rubbed my hands with glee. Pierre had observed the exchange in stunned silence. He had just found out that his superior wasn't as morally superior after all.

'Don't look so shocked, Pierre. All middle-aged Parisian men have mistresses. The wife probably has someone on the side too,' I said, twisting the knife.

'I do *not* have a mistress, Cameron! Stop all this nonsense and let's get back to some actual crimes,' Jean-Claude said, trying to sound firm. I could see he was fuming.

'You're always judging me and it turns out you're no angel yourself,' I said smugly.

'Big difference between murdering someone and cheating on your wife!' said Pierre, coming to his boss's aid and giving me an incredulous look. Jean-Claude gave up denying the affair at this point and calmed himself down, getting back to professional mode and doing his best to appear unperturbed by the mischievous vampire.

'They've found the body of the priest. It was buried where you said it would be,' said Jean-Claude, moving swiftly on.

'So, as I've been a good boy, can I have my picture back?' I asked, hopefully.

'No,' he replied.

'What crimes did you commit after 1993?' asked Pierre, keen to get back to business too.

'I'm only going to tell you about the murders! If we go into all my crimes we'll never finish!'

'Yes, ok. Continue,' he sighed.

As I'd told them, the 1990s were a prosperous time. I had learned enough by then to stay out of trouble. The clubs and pubs were always full of holidaying girls who wanted to enjoy themselves and I had little trouble convincing them to drink champagne and come back to my fabulous apartment overlooking the port. It wasn't until 1998 that I ran into some bother when I got into a fight in a nightclub. I had chatted up a blonde girl that I thought looked a bit cheap in her short skirt, but she had eagerly accepted the glass of champagne I'd offered her and giggled at my lame jokes, so I thought she'd be an easy conquest and a tasty meal. Suddenly, an aggressive guy with slicked back hair and a pale blue shell-suit had forced himself between us. He'd shouted something about getting my filthy hands off his girlfriend and had taken a swing at me. I blocked his arm and hit him in the face. I broke his nose and let the bouncers throw us both out. The girl was pleading with me to leave Jean-Baptiste alone as his nose was bleeding heavily. I did leave them alone and walked away quickly – the sight of all that blood was way too tempting.

I thought that would be the end of the matter, but Jean-Baptiste had had other ideas. He must have spent many nights trawling the local clubs and bars looking for me. When he finally did find me, he waited for me to leave, hiding in a quiet back street armed with a baseball bat. Of course the insulted lover didn't stand a chance and he was found the next morning with his throat slit and with his wallet and a few litres of blood missing.

I'd been worried that this particular murder might come back to haunt me. Our fight had been rather public and there had been countless witnesses, but the man was a small-time, local gangster and his temper and vindictiveness had made me only one minor suspect amongst many, so the police never did knock on my door.

We wrapped our session up for the day and the agents went to check on this latest morsel of information.

Chapter 10: Benoît

Being the restrained vampire I believed myself to be, there weren't many more murders to tell them about, so the interviews became shorter and less frequent and they started to leave me to my own devices for days at a time. I think they were struggling to find a long term solution for me. They couldn't place me in a regular prison and I was obviously too dangerous to let go. After about three months of incarceration, things got really bad. Apart from the little nibble on Jean-Claude, I'd had no human blood since my arrival. Every time the cell door opened I felt the sensation I used to get when I walked past a bakery as a boy. The smell of freshly baked bread would awaken a warm sense of desire and I'd stop and inhale deeply, gazing at all the cakes I desperately wanted but couldn't afford. Now, when the cell door opened, I started to salivate involuntarily. The morning Gaston cut himself shaving almost made me delirious and I was distracted and grumpy during the whole interview that followed. They'd cut the session short, feeling they were getting nowhere with me that day. Blondie was safe with me: I wasn't hungry – I just had a maddening craving for 'cake'.

Being in the cell by myself didn't get any easier. Things in the outside world now seemed so much more attractive than when I was amongst them. I imagined being at one of my friend Andrei's parties. He was a Russian millionaire I had befriended in Cannes and always threw the best shindigs. I imagined being there on his yacht on a warm summer's night, under a star-spangled sky. The champagne would be flowing and we'd be rubbing shoulders with celebrities. I reminisced about all the champagne-sozzled lovelies that I could have taken my pick from, and decided to try my imaginary luck with Hollywood actress Jennifer Lawrence. This being a fantasy she, of course, said yes! Back on my yacht, I poured her another glass of champagne.

'So Jennifer, ever thought of doing a vampire movie?' I asked hoping she was a fan.

This being *my* fantasy, she gushed, 'Vampires are sooo cool! If the right script came along I would love to do a vampire movie!'

'Do you think vampires actually exist?' I asked.

'I'm convinced of it!' she said enthusiastically 'There must be some truth to all these myths and legends. I would *love* to meet one.'

'And would you let him bite you?'

'It's one of my darkest fantasies,' she confessed, leaning into me and giggling.

At this point I sprang my fangs and she let out a small scream, but then she offered me her beautiful neck. I wasn't going to put two puncture marks in her flawless skin, so I went for her equally pristine ankle. She swooned, falling back on the cushions of my sofa while I drank that sweet liquid. I imagined tasting stardust in her blood.

The next day I asked for a DVD of *The Hunger Games* so I could relive my dream. That bastard Jean-Claude had the audacity to suggest that I wanted to watch it for the killing of children! *One more such remark and we'll see just how strong that bullet-proof glass is JC!*

I dreamed of swimming in the Mediterranean, the warm seawater on my skin, but now there were dolphins jumping over my head and attractive mermaids perched on rocky outcrops. They would wave to me and sing with the most beautiful voices. I was slowly losing the plot.

Then there was Emmy. Ever since I had first set eyes on her she'd been the fantasy that had kept me occupied during long daylight hours. When I'd met her in Monaco she had just finished university and was enjoying her last summer of freedom. She was blonde and suntanned and had a body perfected by a healthy and sporty lifestyle. I'd felt very attracted to this young woman that was so full of life, and the fact that she was forbidden fruit only made me desire her more. George had told me in no uncertain terms that he would kill me if I ever touched his daughter. By now, though, I would be happy to die for just one kiss from her sweet lips.

Over the months, my fantasies about Emmy had become more and more elaborate until she had become a full-blown obsession. In the long boring hours alone in my cell I could think of little else. When boys are alone in the dark with nothing to do, their attention naturally turns to making their own amusement. Fantasising about George's daughter was now my main entertainment, though Monique would sometimes make an appearance clad entirely in leather with thigh-high boots... Of course, fantasies are no substitute for the real thing and they served only to make my craving for a real woman worse.

There wasn't a hope in hell that Monique would want to run off with me, but I was definitely going to see Emmy again and do my utmost to seduce her. It had been a long time and I had begun to feel that I could handle letting a woman into my life again. I wanted a girlfriend and she already knew exactly who and what I was. It would be the perfect relationship. I had it all planned out, her accepting me into her heart and us happily living ever after. I even imagined that George would come round and accept me as his son-in-law once he saw how happy we were together. The lack of human blood, being locked up and the distinct lack of mental stimulation was making me seriously delusional.

I tried hard to keep in touch with reality, mainly by attempting interaction with the guards, but Pierre and Jean-Claude never wanted a normal conversation and talking non-stop about myself hardly kept me in touch with reality. I noticed that I was embellishing my stories more and more and remembering things as being a lot more fun and fantastical than they really had been.

The only guards that would talk to me were Gaston and Benoît. One night I was on the roof with both of them. Gaston, short and stocky with cropped brown hair was the older of the two, and I estimated him to be about 50. His face hinted at an interesting but not always easy life. Benoît was just over six foot, my height, and I guessed he was in his mid-thirties. He was handsome in a rugged kind of way, with unruly dark hair and I swore I could actually see his beard grow during the day – by noon his chin had already sprouted a five o'clock shadow. We shared cigarettes and chatted.

'Do you guys have families?'

'My two kids are both grown up now,' said Gaston. 'Actually, I just had my first grandchild.'

'How is the little guy?' asked Benoît. 'Have you got any more photos?'

Now I hate baby pictures. Babies all look the same to me. But when Gaston showed me a picture of little François, I was taken aback and before I could stop myself I blurted out, 'Good *god*, he's ugly!'

'You can't say that!' cried Benoît. 'All babies are beautiful!'

Gaston just laughed. 'He is ugly alright, but my wife and I are hopeful he will grow into those big ears.'

'What about you, Benoît? Any family?' Hastily I added,

'Best not to show me any baby pictures.'

'Married with two daughters, but the girls are not yet old enough for you,' he said threateningly.

'I don't know how I managed to get such a reputation. I've always been a perfect gentleman!'

'See, this is your problem Cameron,' said Gaston pointing his finger accusingly at me. 'There's an enormous difference between how you see yourself and how others see you.'

'Maybe that really is his problem – he can't take a look at himself because he doesn't have a reflection,' said Benoît, onlyhalf joking.

I stubbed out my cigarette and jogged around deep in thought. They too thought I had lost touch with reality. Spending so much time alone, with so little human contact and stimulation was only going to make things worse and I didn't know how much longer I'd be able to hold on to my sanity and keep my baser instincts in check. The last three months had been a lot harder than I could have imagined and I was learning a lot about myself. A thin veneer of the Cameron of old now covered a creature that was driven by a lust for blood and increasingly hard to control.

***

Then one morning, Benoît and another guard came to get me for my gym session and I got another, much stronger, whiff of that fresh bakery smell. Lots of new aromas floated in the air and the whole place just smelled overwhelmingly good. It was obviously a special day, so I asked Benoît what was going on.

'What do you mean?' he asked me bewildered.

'There are other people in the building,' I said, my stomach rumbling alarmingly, 'all young and a few female.'

84

'We're giving some new recruits a day at head office to see how it functions,' he explained. 'Don't tell me you smelled them!'

I nodded and asked him hopefully, 'Will I get to meet some of the new bloods?'

'Certainly not!' he said, clutching his gun. 'Looking at you today, even I have my doubts about being in the service. We don't want to scare these fresh-faced innocents off!'

Benoît had begun to know me well. At this point I wanted nothing other than to rampage through the building, devouring new recruits. To hell with the picture, George and everything! The call of the blood was getting louder and louder and I was having to work ever harder at restraining my urges. The rowing machine bore the brunt of my frustration and when it broke, the guards stood off at a distance, nervously pointing their guns at me.

'I think we'd better take you back to your cell now, Cameron.' Benoît, who was normally quite relaxed around me looked distinctly nervous. 'I'll ask if the psychiatrist can have a word with you. You're mostly a bit calmer after her visit.'

'What I *need* are some volunteers for a blood donation. I'm not crazy, just hungry!' I said angrily, picking up the heaviest weights and starting to juggle furiously with them.

'Can you put those down, please? I'll plead your case, but I think it best we go back to the cells now,' insisted Benoît.

I decided to oblige as I liked Benoît and trusted him to put in a good word for me. I didn't appreciate it but I understood why the dog was no longer in the cell when they brought me back – Blondie would have been toast with me in this mood.

I don't know how Benoît wangled it, but a bag of donor blood turned up a few hours later. I was like a man crawling out of the desert, nearly crying at the sight of the desperately longed for drink. I gulped the healing liquid greedily, before tearing the plastic bag open to lick off every last drop. I had a brief moment of pure happiness and felt I could face the world again without committing mass murder.

***

'Monique darling, you look wonderful this morning!' I chirped when I was taken to her the next day.

'Glad you're back to your cheerful old self, Cameron!' she replied, smiling but then quickly turning serious and professional. 'I heard you had a difficult time yesterday. The guards were concerned that you might attack them. Can you tell me what happened?'

'It's really quite simple: deny a vampire human blood and he will go quite crazy after a while. We have strong urges that just build and build, and if they don't get quenched we eventually snap.'

'Are you feeling calmer now?'

'A little bit, but there is another urge building that needs serious relief,' I said, winking at her. 'You lot managed to get a bag of donor blood, so I'm sure a hooker must be a possibility...'

She didn't flinch. 'The problem is Cameron, that we can't put civilians in harm's way. We have no idea what you will do, though we are certainly starting to get an idea of what you could do.'

'I'll be gentle as a lamb with the professional, I promise!' I said hopefully, but I could see their point.

'Would it help if we got you some adult DVDs and magazines?'

'Oh, yes, please!' I wasn't going to pass up on porn, and it

86

certainly wouldn't hurt. However, I was now thoroughly convinced that Emmy was pining for me too. I had to get out of here soon.

Monique was nice and I enjoyed talking to an intelligent woman, but she wanted to get to know me only so the service could control me better. I was desperate for a relationship without ulterior motives. Emmy, I was sure, would take me as I was; she wouldn't restrain me or try and get into my head only to use it later. She would understand me, support me, and we would be blissfully happy.

'You seemed very far away for a moment there, Cameron. Do you want to tell me about it?'

'I miss the outside world and all the things that go with it.'

'It looked like you were having a fond memory there. What was it?'

'Just thinking about a party I had on a yacht once,' I said, vaguely.

'Do you ever feel guilty about the lives you have taken?'

'Way to put a damper on our little chat! But no, I don't. I mean, everybody has to die eventually. *I* died when I was 19! The world moved on and people forgot.'

'You're still quite bitter about dying and about your family denying your existence. Is that what makes you kill?' she asked.

'I rarely kill, Monique. You make it sound like I'm some psychologically damaged, deranged serial killer! If I kill, it's to avoid detection or for revenge, but mostly it's the hunger.'

'Don't you see that it is wrong?'

'Monique! Stop thinking you can cure me! What you lot are trying to do is like trying to turn a lion into a vegetarian. Can you imagine asking him if he had any regrets about killing that beautiful gazelle!'

'Except Cameron, that you are a rational being. You have a choice not too kill,' she argued.

I was getting fed up with everyone wanting me to behave according to human standards. I believed I was more akin to a majestic predator. 'Just like a tiger, if I'm fed and treated right you might have a manageable cat on your hands. Whatever else goes on in my head is my business and won't change the fact that I'm a wild animal – wild majestic and beautiful – but if you don't feed me appropriately, or if you deny me a mate, I'll bite your head off!'

I regretted it as soon as I said it; she was the last person I wanted to threaten. I was frustrated and her prodding about in my brain wasn't helping. She didn't say anything for a while, and then she looked at me with a despondent look of pity.

'I'll get you those DVDs and then we'll have another talk in a few days,' she said eventually.

I wanted to tell her that I would never bite her head off, but instead I just nodded my head. I was doing very badly in here; I was not making any friends and I felt more alone than ever.

***

When I came back from my gym session the next day, I noticed a jar on my desk. I approached it curiously as it was an odd thing to have placed in my cell. It was filled with rice, which was even weirder as I couldn't imagine what they thought I'd want with uncooked rice. I sat on the bed staring at the jar. *What are they up to now?*

I got up and went over to have a closer look. I've always been very tidy. I like to fold things and put them in their right place and when I arrange my things I count them without even noticing I'm doing it. Counting is something that grounds and calms me. When I'm upset I often tear bits of paper and while I like to pretend it's the destruction that calms me down, it's really counting the snippets of paper that does the trick. *I wonder how many grains are in there?* I opened the jar, tipped the rice on to the desk and started counting. But counting them once was not enough; I had to lay the grains out in neat rows and groups of ten. The table proved too small and I moved to the floor. I snarled at Blondie when she started showing an interest in the little grains, she whimpered and beat a hasty retreat on to the bed with her tail between her legs, I cursed and started over again.

I was surprised when I heard the cell door open and they came to get me for my morning exercise. I hadn't even realised they'd left me in my cell for nearly 24 hours and it was the next day. Time had flown by and I hadn't even thought about feeding. Feeling less enthusiastic than usual, I did my exercises somewhat lethargically, had a shower and was taken back to my cell. I was relieved to see that the jar was still sitting in the same place but I didn't trust them. *What if they've removed a few grains?* I told myself not to be so idiotic and to ignore the jar, but during the afternoon interview I could think of little else. I was dying to get back to my cell to count the rice.

I was right to have been worried. The bastards had removed five grains! From that moment on, the jar didn't leave my sight. I was pissed off that I'd given them another bargaining tool, but I couldn't control my own silly obsession.

'So what's up with this fucking rice thing?' I started my next session with Monique.

'You seemed very upset and out of sorts at our last meeting. I thought I'd do some research into vampire habits according to different legends, as I didn't seem to be getting anywhere with my usual methods. Something that comes up time and time again in stories is the vampire's obsession with counting things. Call it OCD or obsessive compulsive behaviour,' she explained, looking a little guilty.

'In some countries they put grains of rice in the coffin when they bury the dead. Allegedly, if the body wakes up as a vampire he or she will be too busy counting the rice to bother coming out of the grave,' she went on, annoying me with her new-found knowledge. 'In others they hang colanders on their doors thinking the vampire will be so obsessed with counting the holes he'll forget to come in and may even get caught out in the rising sun.'

'Oh how very interesting!' I snapped, crossly.

'I was amazed by the similarity between all the legends, so I thought there might be some truth in it,' she said slyly. 'I hate to have experimented on you like that, but something was needed and I was running out of ideas with human psychology.'

'So you're just going to throw grains and tiny items in my cell in the hope it will pacify me?' I was outraged that they'd found me so easy. *How dare you manipulate me!*

'When is the last time you fed?'

I hadn't fed since the first jar had appeared. When I'd started carrying that about with me, another jar was put in my cell. On the desk in front of me now were five jars of rice. *Five days!*

'It's been five days you manipulative bitch!' I said, grabbing my stomach. I realised it was hurting and I'd just been able to ignore it while I was obsessing over my jars. I'd thought I was a strong-willed individual and I was furious that she had me on my knees with a stupid folklore trick.

90

'Well, you'll be pleased to know there will be no more jars appearing in your cell.'

'Really? Why?' I asked, astonished.

'Jean-Claude complained to me that you have been distracted and unco-operative in your interviews.'

'Oh?'

'Seems that you can't wait to get back to your cell these days, and when they ask you questions you often don't answer as you're too busy examining your jars.'

'Hmm,' I almost growled.

'Do you want to keep the jars you have?'

I sat in silence thinking for quite a while. As much as I wanted to keep the jars, I had to show her I was stronger than that and that she couldn't tame me so easily. I grabbed the jars and threw them one by one in her direction, making them smash against the bulletproof glass. Now I was sitting amongst a mass of broken glass and rice and the temptation to fall to my knees on the floor was so strong I feared my head would explode. For a few moments we both sat trembling in our chairs. Then, not wanting to look at her or the rice any more, I turned round and stared at the blank white wall doing my best not to look at the floor. I held steady until the guards came to return me to my cell. I hoped with all my heart that they were done with leaving jars of rice in there.

For a few days after, I was out of sorts and obsessing about rice in spite of myself, but at least I was able to feed again. It's true what they say: out of sight out of mind. Slowly, things returned to normality. Jean-Claude was pleased that I was paying attention to what they were saying again and even though I was feeding from her, the dog seemed happier too, as she was getting my attention again. She bounced around the cell like a daft thing, barking with excitement when I took out the tennis ball.

Clearly, I was going to have to work a lot harder at fighting my urges, but it would be no small challenge. I played with the dog and heartily wished I was her.

Chapter 11: George

One morning, a few days after the rice experiment ended, a guard came in with the newspapers and as per usual I read the first page of the *Daily Mail* and then turned over for the sports, followed by the obituaries. One of the announcements made me sit up with a start: 'George Baxter', it read.

After a moment's reflection, I realised I didn't feel upset. In fact, I was thinking *Ya fucking beauty!* George knew that I made a habit of reading the obituaries and I realised that he had probably placed the advert himself as an invitation for me to flee. Not that I'd have been too upset if he had died. I liked George – I mean I'd cared enough to hand myself in for him – but I was under no illusions. Humans die eventually and I'd been around long enough that death no longer upset me. In fact, if the old bastard really had kicked the bucket, Emmy wouldn't be off-limits any more! Also the rice experiment had rattled me profusely. They might have stopped for now while they still wanted to get information from me, but what would stop them from trying other experiments in the future? No matter what, I had to get out of here.

And so I started plotting my escape from the DCRI headquarters. In the time that I had been there I had only seen five different armed guards, but I knew there were lots of other people in the building. I could smell them. I hadn't been able to get a good grasp of the building's layout as I was only ever taken to three locations: the interview room, the gym and the rooftop. At all times I had two armed guards with me, but even though they had guns, I knew I'd be able to get to them before they could get a shot on target. I started to pay a lot more attention to who was guarding me when.

Later that morning I was led to the gym by Luc and Cyrille, both very serious, professional agents who didn't seem to have much of a sense of humour. Both were monosyllabic if I tried to strike up a conversation. They were actually quite similar looking: short, blond hair, square chins and built like brick shithouses. I was pretty sure they worked out together and that acquiring bigger muscles was their main aim in life. I enjoyed lifting weights in front of them, ones that they could only ever dream of lifting.

Benoît, on the other hand, was more human. We'd continued to have a smoke and a laugh together when he escorted me to the rooftop. He was one of the few who treated me like a normal person. At one point he had even laid his gun nonchalantly on the wall and sat down on the floor with a cigarette.

When I'd raised my eyebrows he'd told me calmly, 'If you wanted to leave, a gun wouldn't stop you, would it Cameron?'

I'd smiled and done another 30 one-handed push-ups to show him he was right. His young colleague, Henri, had watched us nervously, holding very tightly on to his own gun. I imagined he was just out of the academy and this was likely to be his first posting. They probably didn't teach new recruits how to deal with vampires and he was evidently very unsure of himself.

'Relax Henri. Cameron here isn't going to do anything. By the way, what have they got over you that you're staying?' Benoît had asked me.

'Friend of mine will go back to prison if I run,' I'd told him.

'Big bad vampire like you cares about friends?' he'd asked me mockingly.

'I can be very loyal to the people that don't piss me off!'

'And the people that do piss you off?' he'd asked, dragging on his cigarette.

'Let's just say I neither forgive nor forget.'

Taking a final drag, he'd stood up and crushed the butt out with his heel. 'Sorry Cameron, time's up. We need to take you back in. Hope that doesn't put me on your revenge list?'

'Nah, you're just doing your job. Now Jean-Claude, on the other hand, has been a total dick. I might need to bite him again.'

Benoît had giggled and when Henri was out of earshot had murmured, 'You're not wrong; he is a bit of a dick.'

The fifth guard was a few years older than the others and reminded me a lot of George as he had an army background and had seen things no man should ever have to see. He didn't mind talking to me if we were on the rooftop and he had some great stories from his army days. He had been to many places, but he told me he was planning to move to Tahiti upon his retirement. In my previous life, I would love to have had Gaston on my team, and I'm sure he would've enjoyed rescuing hostages.

I decided that the rooftop would be the easiest place to escape from and I'd make sure neither Gaston nor Benoît were on duty. Henri was clearly the weakest link and with his youth and inexperience would be the easiest to overrun. I would have to kill the two guards and then jump to the nearby trees, which would hopefully break my fall well enough for me to be able to run off to the Metro station. Once in the underground, I'd be impossible to find.

***

After my gym session, at about 11 o'clock, I was led back to the interview room.

'Good morning, gentlemen! You're in luck today; I'm in an excellent mood. I may even tell you a few truths!' I started off cheerfully.

'And *why* are you in such a great mood?' asked Jean-Claude suspiciously.

'I just am,' I said beaming. 'I hope you are too, as I'm willing to trade for the picture.'

'Apprehension of another vampire would get you the picture back,' stated Jean-Claude.

'That's not entirely fair! Actually catching a vampire would depend on you lot being skilful enough to bring one in. I handed myself in, so I'm not convinced you have what it takes.'

'Give us enough so we can at least have a shot.'

I wasn't going to give them Carl-Heinz, the poor guy had spent too much time locked up already. Nanette had probably moved on and I had no idea where she was, but I had an idea of how to find her. I decided I would throw Nanette to the dogs – after three months of prison, my freedom and the picture had come to mean more to me.

'I can try and give you Nanette,' I proposed.

'So she *is* a vampire?' asked Pierre.

'Yep. Not a very old one, but I would still be wary of her.'

'Do you know her real name?' inquired Jean-Claude.

'She goes by the name of Nanette Weisman and she pretends to be the wife of millionaire Harold Weisman III, but she wasn't actually married to him and it's likely he's dead by now. Her real name is Wided Medjnoun and she told me she still uses the original paperwork with that name.'

'We traced her IP address to Harold Weisman's house, and you're right. He is dead and Nanette is long gone,' said Pierre.

'We didn't know her real name, though, so we can start with that.'

The interview was stopped at this point and the men left probably to send messages out to police and other authorities. After a few hours back in my cell, they asked me to sit with a sketch artist again, as they had no pictures of Nanette. Of course I didn't tell them about the picture I had found in the papers when the Marseillaise police were looking for missing prostitute Wided Medjnoun; getting a sketch artist to do a portrait was way more fun.

I asked him to show me a few tricks as I had moved on from drawing the dog and was trying to do portraits from memory. I had my nose pressed up against the glass as he worked, utterly fascinated by his skill. He did a stunning likeness of Nanette and I almost felt guilty for handing them such a good portrait, but not for long. Nanette could handle herself and would cause mayhem if they tried to catch her. I asked him to do me next and as we had been left alone, he did a quick portrait of me. I was amazed. It was just like looking in a mirror nearly a hundred years ago. I hadn't changed at all physically. Staring back at me was the young man that had gone off to war, except that the haircut was awful. They didn't want to subject any civilians to danger so Jean-Claude had assured me that Henri the junior agent was quite adept at cutting hair. I was a little suspicious, but Henri told me his dad was a barber and it felt like he knew what he was doing. It was now clear that they had all lied. I was impressed though, that Henri had the guts to risk getting so thoroughly on my bad side, unless he really did think he could cut hair... But I had to let it slide, as I was focused fully on escaping. I had enough reasons already to hate Jean-Claude bitterly and Henri was on the kill list anyway.

Before the end of the day, the two agents came back in for another chat.

'She could, of course, have changed her name. I did give her my papers contact,' I said, trying to sound even more helpful.

'We would like that guy too,' said Jean-Claude.

I wasn't keen on that idea as I'd be likely to need him again and he and I got on like a house on fire.

'That would be difficult. He never has clients come to his workshop. I leave him a message and then he calls me and we meet in a public place.' Nonsense, of course: I knew exactly which backstreet of Marseille he worked from. We had known each other for some years and if ever I needed documents, I would go and see him. We were even Facebook friends and he'd often post pictures of cats merely because he knew I couldn't stand them.

'I can set up a call with him and see if he did any papers for her,' I volunteered. I could leave a mutual friend a message on Facebook asking him to call me. He'd be suspicious enough to use a burner cell phone, so they wouldn't be able to trace him from the call.

They agreed to let me have internet access just to post the message. A laptop was brought in and I shuffled in my seat in anticipation as I logged in. I rapidly scrolled through all the postings since I had disappeared, and it gave me a warm feeling to read all the messages from my Facebook friends mourning my death and expressing general disbelief in my guilt. Jean-Claude eventually told me to get on with it and post the message immediately. I didn't send Hamid – my document contact – the message, but asked one of our mutual friends to pass it on. Hopefully I had done enough to protect him. As soon as I clicked the send button Jean-Claude took the laptop away from me, despite my growling.

They then left me alone for the night, as it was already quite late and they didn't think Hamid would call straight away. Calls on the mobile they'd left me would be recorded and a trace started as soon as it rang. I tried to do a portrait of Nanette as well that night, using the techniques the artist had shown me, but mine was awful compared with his. I put my art materials away and made up a rota with the times and days the different guards were on. It didn't change very often and I soon figured out that a Friday night would present the best escape opportunity. That gave me another five days to get my painting back. I lay back on the bed, plotting.

Chapter 12: Hamid

The guards came to get me for my gym session at about eight o'clock the following morning and I was pleased to see that Luc and Gaston were on duty as per my rota. At around noon the mobile suddenly rang and I received a call from Hamid.

'Hello,' I said, as Jean-Claude and Luc rushed into my cell.

'A'salaamu aleikum,' the Arabic greeting came over the line when I answered the call.

'Aleikum a'salaam, Hamid my man. It's Cameron here. How are you?' I started the call in my usual jovial manner.

'I'm well, praise be to Allah.' I saw the agents looking very interested. If they thought I was giving them a fanatical religious terrorist they were wrong. Hamid was motivated purely by money, but figured it couldn't do any harm to praise Allah now and then.

'Not seen you for a long time, Cameron. What are you up to? I even heard rumours you were dead?'

'Someone is out to get me, framing me for a murder Hamid. I just had to disappear for a while.'

'That's heavy man. Who's after you?'

'Business rival who wanted me off his patch,' I lamented.

'It's always the nicest guys that that sort of shit happens to,' he replied, sarcastically.

'I *know*! You try to make a decent living and some fucker frames you for murder!' Out of the corner of my eye I saw Jean-Claude with some headphones on, staring at me, his eyes narrowed and arms folded impatiently. I imagined cartoon smoke coming from his ears. I cheerfully pointed at the phone and then gave him a thumbs up.

'So, what can I do for you?' Hamid asked.

'Did that woman Nanette that I recommended ever contact you?'

'Yes, about a month ago. I gave her a new passport.'

'I'm trying to trace her. I need her help on a wee job, but she's keeping her head down,' I told him. 'You wouldn't remember the name on that passport would you?'

'She's actually still in Marseille. I'll get her to give you a call if I see her.'

What the hell is she doing in Marseille? 'Why is she still there?' I asked surprised.

'Not sure Cam, she wouldn't tell me, but she seemed to be very interested in this guy Karim. You must know him. He runs a couple of brothels and other shit,' Hamid told me.

I was stunned. I'd never figured that Nanette would want to go back to her old life. Maybe she was running the show this time, but I couldn't see how she could keep a violent thug like Karim in line and not be discovered as a vampire. This was all very puzzling.

'Yes, get her to call me. You have my number.' We exchanged some more pleasantries and I ended the call a few minutes later.

'So I suppose we just have to wait now, but I've got Nanette on the radar for you!' I said looking pleased with myself.

'It's a very promising lead. We'll circulate her description to the authorities in Marseille,' said Jean-Claude getting up.

'I wouldn't do that,' I warned. 'She is extremely dangerous. You don't want some bright-eyed young copper trying to arrest her and getting his head bitten off now, do you?'

'We'll just ask them to follow her at a distance if they spot her, until we can get a team in place,' said Jean-Claude.

They had a lot of information to work with so I was left to wait in my cell. Someone was posted outside with the mobile in case Nanette called. I was disappointed in her. It seemed ridiculous that she'd want to go back to a life of crime and prostitution after living the high life in Cannes. It made no sense to me at all. Anybody dealing with the Marseille underworld had heard of Karim. He'd grown up in one of the schemes on the outskirts of the city and joined a gang when he was only 11, starting as a lookout for the local dealers, but working his way up to dealing and petty crime. It was alleged that Karim held the fastest time record in Marseille for stealing a Renault Clio.

His younger brothers, Sofiane and Ahmed, had followed in his footsteps. As a minor, Karim had been up on drugs charges a couple of times and while locked up had learned how to become a proper hardened criminal. By the age of 17 he was doing armed robberies. When he turned 18, and could be tried as an adult, he disappeared suddenly, but bodies soon started piling up. Karim and his brothers turned violently on their former patrons and took over the gang and, from then on, Karim worked smarter, preferring to stay in the background while others did the dirty work. By the time I'd first heard of him in 2004, he and his brothers had built up an impressive network running drugs, guns and prostitution. I suppose if Nanette was going to align herself with anyone, he wasn't a bad option, if very, very dangerous. We vampires weren't invincible: the simple act of opening the curtains could hurt and unveil us.

I heard the mobile going, the door opened and a young agent rushed in to hand me the phone.

'Nanette darling. Thanks for calling!' I smiled, thinking of poor Didier tapping away like mad in the other room trying to record two vampires chewing the fat.

'What do you want, Dogbreath?'

'Come, come baby vampire. Play nice.'

'If you call me that again, I'll hang up!' she snarled.

'What are you doing in Marseille? Rumour has it you've taken up your old trade?'

'None of your business. Now what do you want?' *Shit what do I want?* I hadn't thought of a cover story!

'Can I call you back? I'm kind of in the middle of something,' I asked, my mind a complete blank as to how to coax her out.

'There's a girl with you, isn't there?'

'Yes and she's looking bored,' I whispered. 'I don't want her losing interest now.'

'Fine, call me when you're done,' she said and hung up.

I sat on the bed holding the mobile and looked up at the agent.

'I don't think that was long enough for a trace, Cameron,' he said.

'Well this is a bit of a cock-up. You lot could have briefed me before I took the call. Where do you want this woman?' I retorted, annoyed.

'Call her back and see if she'll agree to meet you,' he suggested.

I hadn't met this agent before. They probably put the least bright sparks on the night shift.

'Why would I want to see her? What can she do for me?' I asked, despairing.

'*I* don't know! What do you vampires do when you get together? Trade virgins or something?' the young agent stammered.

'Trade virgins…?'

'Well you tell me! I don't know what you get up to apart from drinking blood and killing people!' He looked flustered.

'I think I'd better call Jean-Claude.'

'Yes. You do that,' I said, waving him away.

It was ten o'clock at night, so Jean-Claude wouldn't be pleased to receive a call so late at home, but he arrived at my cell just half an hour later.

'Did he get you at home or at your mistress's?' I asked gleefully.

He gave me a dirty look but didn't answer. 'Ask her for the alarm code to her old house. We know the place has been sold but there are now new, wealthy owners. Say you're willing to split the profits if she helps you with the security.'

'Not bad,' I said, admiringly. 'She might just go for that.'

'See if she wants to meet to go over the plan, say you managed to get blueprints to the house,' Jean-Claude went on.

'She's going to be livid if you catch her. You'd be best just to stake her straight away!' I suggested, thinking more of my own hide. She'd instantly know that I'd set her up and would hunt me to the ends of the earth in revenge. I was sure of that.

'No. We still have a lot to learn about your kind. She could lead us to others and solve a few murders and missing persons cases too.'

'Trust me. I'm here entirely by choice. If you don't kill her first, she will rip you to shreds,' I urged.

He looked suitably worried. He'd seen mere glimpses of my abilities, but they had scared him enough to take note of my warning now.

'We'll consider that. Give her a call now and set up a meeting.' He handed me the phone.

I did as he asked. 'Nanette, darling. Your favourite vampire again!'

'Was she tasty?'

'You know I always enjoy Italian food and she was from

Naples. What did you have for dinner?' I babbled away merrily.

'About to have more overweight scumbag in a little while,' she said grimly.

'I really don't understand why you are back in Marseille,' I probed again.

'You went back to Scotland eventually to look into your family, well I've done the same. Like yourself I had a few demons to put to rest,' she explained.

'How are your relatives? Where they pleased to see you?' I chirped.

'Don't be an idiot. I just made inquiries and I found my sister's youngest is in trouble.'

'Ah, now it makes more sense that you're hunting down Karim,' I said. 'Have you found your niece yet?'

'Yes, hence the overweight scumbag on the menu.'

So we'd have to move fast. After dealing with the family crisis, Nanette wouldn't want to hang around Marseille for long. I spun her the story about wanting to do the burglary and she agreed to meet me.

'Where are you, Cameron? I thought you were in Germany?'

'No I'm back in Paris, so you'll have to give me a few days to get down there.'

'It was rather clever, confessing and faking your own death' she said. 'How did you manage that?'

'Wasn't it! My friend George always had very useful contacts,' I said, avoiding a direct answer.

She wanted to meet in a bar in the 15th Arrondissement, but Jean-Claude shook his head. He and his men would immediately be sussed out in what was a police no-go area.

'You know Marseille, Nanette, a pale baby face like mine

always ends up in trouble in those neighbourhoods. Can we meet in the centre where I can mix with tourists and not stand out?'

'I thought you rather liked getting into fights with bad elements,' she said, amused.

'Not when I want to conduct business.' We agreed on a bar near the Vieux Port in the centre of Marseille and I hung up.

'Great. We can work with that. Good night, Cameron, I'll see you tomorrow.' With that Jean-Claude left hastily, keen to get back home... or back to his mistress.

Chapter 13: Nanette

'I think you should let me go and stake her,' I told the two agents first thing the next day.

'We want her alive, Cameron,' said Pierre.

'You're going to need lots of silver, netting, cuffs etc. She is not going to go down easily!' I warned them. 'Honestly, it would be better to kill her.' I didn't care how many throats she was going to rip open, I didn't want her coming after me once I was out. 'Well, don't say I didn't warn you. You know, unlike humans, vampire females are a lot stronger than males,' I said, nicely playing down my own abilities and having a last ditch attempt at being allowed to kill her.

The two agents looked rather unconvinced.

'Really? Female vampires are stronger than males? Why would that be?' asked Jean-Claude, the idea of the female sex being physically stronger was unthinkable to such a conservative stick in the mud.

'I dunno. They just are.' I replied. It could be true. I'd never had the urge to arm wrestle with Nanette and find out.

'We'll make sure we have all precautions in place and we'll see you when we get back,' said Jean-Claude.

'Can I have my picture before you go in case you don't make it back? I did give you Nanette and I would hate to think of you two lying dead in Marseille and no one knowing the code to the safe.'

'A, someone does know how to get it and B, I fully intend to be here in a few days to give you your painting,' said Jean-Claude confidently, and he brought the interview to a close.

'Pierre, put your affairs in order,' I said ominously, as I was led back to my cell. I knew how deadly we vampires could be when driven into a corner.

'We'll take all possible precautions, Cameron,' he assured me. 'Being an agent is always dangerous, so my affairs are in order. But I fully intend to make it back here.'

I was left by myself for the most part after that, though I still got to go to the gym in the morning and to the roof at night. I spotted that most of the armed guards remained and only Gaston seemed to be absent. It made sense that they'd put a man with his military background on the team sent to track Nanette down. On the night of the mission, I found myself on the roof with Benoît.

'I don't think they'll catch her, but if they do never let your guard down with her,' I warned him.

'You don't have much faith in our abilities,' he said, offering me a cigarette.

'Jean-Claude is an idiot and he and apprentice idiot are going to get themselves killed!' I stated glumly. 'You people are just starting to learn about our abilities and I sometimes get the impression you still doubt that I'm real!'

I took the cigarette Benoît had offered and let him light it. He smoked the strong Gauloises and they made me feel light-headed, but I didn't let on in case he thought I was a complete wuss. It was a way to bond and get closer to him. I never understood why narcotics affected me so badly; maybe it was something to do with our borrowing blood from others to keep our dead bodies going. Strangely enough I wasn't too bad on horse tranquilisers, sleeping pills and other chemically produced drugs. *Two unnatural things cancelling each other out?* Maybe it was just bad circulation – that would explain my difficulty with the cold as well – but then again nothing about being a vampire made sense; none of the rules that applied to humans applied to me any longer.

'You should look up "vampires on the western front in World War Two" for a laugh, Benoît. Most of the witness accounts by German soldiers are true; it was me and my old mate George doing our part to liberate you lot,' I said smiling.

'Do you ever get fed up with living?' he asked, suddenly. 'I mean, you have been around for a long time.'

'Not so far. The advances in technology have been amazing to witness and I definitely want to be around when they make hover cars and teleportation devices,' I said enthusiastically. 'There's also a particular German girl I want to have my way with.'

He gave me a probing look and asked, 'So when are you thinking of breaking out of here?'

'I just gave them a big lead. I think they will eventually start to trust me and let me venture out. I could be a great asset to you people. Did I ever tell you I used to rescue hostages?' I chattered away innocently, pretending he hadn't just hit the nail on the head.

'Really? Why would you do that? You don't seem the charitable type?' he asked surprised.

'There's good money in it; first job netted us five million.'

Benoît whistled, impressed.

'It was also one of the few chances I got to truly misbehave,' I added, winking.

'You're sick man!' Benoît said smiling. He stubbed out his cigarette and got up.

'Time to put you back in your cage, Cameron. God I hope you never decide to "misbehave" here,' he said grabbing his gun and gesturing for me to walk ahead.

'Don't worry,' I replied casually.

I was led back to my cell and there I had to sit and wait for news. At eight o'clock I was ready for my gym session and the dog was keen to go out for his exercise too, but the place remained eerily quiet.

'Guess things went pear-shaped in Marseille,' I said to the dog. She sat expectantly by the door, looking burstingly eager to go for her walk. Eventually I banged on the cell door, as I had no desire to share my space with a heap of dog excrement. If they didn't come soon I would have to kill the mutt just to stop the inevitable from happening. At nine o'clock the door opened and Henri arrived to take the dog. He looked visibly upset.

'You will have to stay in your cell today, we are having some security issues,' he said avoiding my eyes.

'Things went tits-up in Marseille, then?' I asked.

'Can't say at this moment. You are requested to stay in your cell,' he said and closed the door hurriedly. He wasn't going to tell me the news.

Fuck, she's on the loose and hating my guts even more!

The dog didn't come back that day. I wasn't too bothered as I had breakfasted and I could imagine that no one wanted to talk to me, but after a second day of no contact or distraction, I started to get seriously fed up. They couldn't just leave me to rot away in this cell! I sized up the door but didn't think I could get out. I contemplated running at the first opportunity – I could always come back later for the painting – and then finally I heard people approaching and the door opened. Grim-faced, Luc and Cyrille asked me to make my way to the interview room.

'I did warn you!' I said trying not to gloat as I sat on the other side of the glass from Pierre.

'Yes you did, and we really didn't appreciate how dangerous she was,' he said. He looked devastated.

'Do you want to tell me about it?' I asked, doing my best to sounding sincerely sympathetic. *Every gory detail please!*

'I'm in the process of writing up my report. I'll let you have a copy when I'm done,' he said. He looked very tired. He couldn't have had much sleep in the last few days, but he'd probably have even greater problems sleeping in the days to follow.

'We need to catch her; she is very dangerous. Can you give us any more information?' I could hear in his voice that he didn't hold out much hope.

'I don't think so. She'll be spooked and pissed off at me. The only way you'll catch her now is if she tries to break in here wielding a big wooden stake with my name on it!'

'*Any* little detail you remember about her, anything at all that might help find her, please tell us Cameron.'

'I will. I don't want her out there either!'

'I'm sorry about keeping you locked in your cell. We'll try to resume normal routines but, at the moment, it's too difficult,' Pierre told me morosely.

'At least give me the dog back!'

'She's already back in your cell and I'll see if there are any volunteers for your roof outing tonight.'

'Ok, so who died,' I asked, as I was just too curious.

'You'll have my report soon.' He got up and the two guards led me back to my cell.

That night, Benoît and Luc took me to the roof, but neither was too talkative: I understood that they wouldn't want to discuss the murder of their colleagues with the likes of me. I had plenty of pent-up energy to get rid of so I was happy enough just to run around for a while. When I got back to my cell I found Pierre's report on my desk. I got comfortable on my bed with the dog snoozing at my side.

***

They had confronted Nanette before she went into the café where we had agreed to meet, 'they' being Pierre, Jean-Claude, Gaston and two Marseille-based agents. According to Pierre they had shown her the silver netting that they'd had made for the mission and she'd agreed to come with them. She'd got calmly in the car, flanked on the back seat by Gaston and Jean-Claude with Pierre driving. She'd let herself be handcuffed and both guards had their service revolvers pressed against her ribs. The two Marseille agents followed closely in a second car, armed with shotguns.

They'd driven at speed away from the centre and towards a holding facility on the outskirts of Marseille. When they were out of the centre and driving through a quieter neighbourhood, Nanette had swiftly and viciously killed the two agents at her side despite both of them getting off a few shots. Pierre had brought the car to a halt while getting his gun out of his holster, but Nanette had got out before the car had even stopped. The three agents had pursued on foot, following the trail of blood, but the trail had dried up after two hundred meters and they'd stopped to bring in a K-9 unit. The dogs couldn't get a scent and didn't get further than where the blood trail stopped. Nanette had vanished without a trace.

She had fed, so her wounds would be healing fast, but I knew the wound of my betrayal would never heal. I put the report down and reflected on how lucky Pierre had been to escape with his life. I was pleased Jean-Claude was dead, but I wished it had been me that killed him. Pierre, I was sure, I'd get on better with.

***

'It's a shame about Gaston,' I said the next morning, commiserating sincerely. 'I did like the guy.'

'Yes, they were both good men,' said Estrosi, giving me a grim look.

I briefly raised my eyebrows indicating that I didn't wholly agree. I was pleased though that the big boss was sitting in with Pierre; they were finally taking things seriously. They knew now how devastatingly dangerous we vampires were. They might still have some doubts as to whether we even existed, but after their run in with Nanette they now knew they had to deal with a very real threat of some kind.

I hadn't liked Estrosi when I'd met him once before and I didn't like him now. He was like Jean-Claude, serious and devoid of humour. He was also one of those people that expressed his authority by shouting and banging tables. I don't react well to bullies, finding that politeness goes further.

'Anything you can give us on Nanette would be helpful,' he started off, calmly enough.

'She hates me now – thanks to you bollocksing up the whole operation. As I said to Pierre, she might well be on her way here with a stake already!'

'Does she have any friends or family were she might hide out?' asked Pierre.

'Nanette doesn't do friends and her family think she's dead. But before I help you any more, I would like you to keep your promises and give me my painting back!' I sat back huffily, crossing my arms.

'We would like to have her in custody first,' said Estrosi, his voice growing a tad louder.

'Fuck you! You had her and you totally ignored my advice!

113

Fuck you! I'm done talking!' I turned my chair round so they could admire my broad shoulders.

'Cameron, please. We need your help here,' pleaded Pierre.

I stuck my middle finger up at them in defiance. I was fuming.

'There are other things we could take away!' shouted Estrosi.

This time they got a two-fingered response. It stayed quiet for a long time and I figured they must have left the room to deliberate about what tack to take. Then suddenly, Pierre's voice piped up again, 'Cameron. Is there *any* information you could give us that could help us catch her?'

'Yes!' I whipped round to face them. *Unlikely!*

'Get him his bloody picture then,' said Estrosi angrily.

Yes, bloody, yes! I waited triumphantly until a nervous looking Henri came in with the small canvas. I looked the picture over lovingly; it was one of Hélène's best works. She had been in love and initially that had brought out the best in her, before it slowly destroyed her. I turned the picture over. It would be easier to lie if that young innocent wasn't staring back at me.

'I don't think Nanette will be hanging around in Marseille,' I started truthfully, 'she would have stolen a car with a big boot and will probably be in Paris by now.' Then I started talking nonsense. 'I gave her another contact if she ever needed papers in Paris.'

I gave them the address of the guy that had made me ID papers in the late 1940s. Maybe the great-grandchildren would be running the business now, but they certainly wouldn't find Nanette there. Hopefully it would keep them busy until the next day. I was going off the roof that night.

114

Chapter 14: Juan

I was excited, but nervous – I knew I wouldn't get another chance if the attempt went wrong. I checked the rota and confirmed that Benoît wasn't due to be on that night, though with Gaston's death I realised that might not be a certainty. I wrapped the canvas in a thin t-shirt and hid it against my stomach, holding it securely in place with another tight fitting t-shirt and my Armani jeans. Then I put on a black turtleneck jumper over the top, which both hid the small bump and made me a less visible target. The guards usually came for me at 11, so at ten I drained the dog – I was going to need all the strength I could muster. When the knock came at the door to my cell, I was delighted to see it was Luc and Cyrille that had come for me.

'Dog gave up the ghost. Better start looking for a new mutt,' I said casually as the door opened.

Luc came into the cell and gave the dog a push with his foot.

'Trust me, I know a dead dog when I see one,' I said to him, with a mischievous grin.

Neither said a word but just gestured for me to leave the room and walk towards the stairs. The door to the stairs wasn't locked so I pushed it open and held it for the agents to go through. I attacked while they were both close to me and therefore unable to get a shot off before I tore open their jugulars. I took their guns off them as they held on to their throats, eyes wide with terror. Then I fed savagely on both of them until there was no more to have. The human blood was even better than I remembered and I felt a warm wave of energy rush through my body. Having wiped myself clean, I went on up to the roof, had a quick look over the edge of the parapet, then stepped back and took a run and a jump to the nearest tree. The branches smashed against my arms and I grasped frantically to get a handhold. As soon as I felt secure, I eased myself slowly down to the pavement, brushed myself off and started jogging to the nearest metro station. Once below ground, I jumped the barrier ignoring the angry shouts from the station staff. A train had just pulled into the station and I got on, waving the furious staff goodbye. I breathed in deeply. Free at last! I knew these tunnels like the back of my hand – they'd never find me down here.

***

Back in the catacombs, I was safe in the maze of tunnels that I could navigate even in the pitch black. I had a very good hiding place where I had once stashed a genuine Picasso for nearly 90 years and where I had left some money and my burglary tools in case I ever needed to escape. I had lost a lot: my boat, most of my money and wardrobe, but I knew I would be on my feet again in no time. I spend the next two days re-exploring the familiar tunnels, to find that where they used to feel safe and comforting they now just reminded me of my cell. I might be able to wander for miles, but I was still surrounded by cold hard walls. As soon as night fell, I ventured above ground in search of prey and a new wardrobe.

I hung around outside a nightclub until I spotted a man who had my build and similarly fine taste. I followed him and was delighted to discover that he was on foot and didn't live too far from the club. I waited until I saw the lights in his apartment go on and then off again after about half an hour. I let myself in when I thought he'd have fallen asleep, heard him snoring from the hallway and followed the noise to his bedroom. I planted my fangs into his neck and drained him of every drop. Having seen the man leave the nightclub alone, I'd decided he was likely to be single and living on his own so I figured I'd have a bit of time to dispose of the body. I switched on the lights and took a look around his apartment.

The man was obviously quite wealthy and, apart from some candlesticks I didn't like, it could've been me that had decorated the place. He had a couple of black leather couches and some interesting modern art on the wall. I put the candlesticks in the kitchen bin and looked through his wardrobe, finding some very nice Armani and Hugo Boss suits. I tried on one of the jackets and found it did indeed fit perfectly. This was wonderful; I had just killed my identical style twin! I closed all the curtains and set to work.

I started packing a couple of large suitcases he had, going systematically through all the wardrobes, cupboards and drawers and packing anything I needed or that had value. Then I found his car keys and discovered a BMW fob on them. I'd really hit the jackpot here! It was still dark, so I ran excitedly down the stairs into the street below, to see if I could locate the car and sure enough, when I pressed the button on the fob a brand new white BMW 5 Series Gran Turismo flashed its lights. *No way! This is just too good! Mind, I'd've preferred it in black...*

And then I started to get worried. This was all going a wee bit too swimmingly for comfort. I went back upstairs shaking my head in disbelief at my good fortune. His Spanish driving licence and passport identified him as one Juan Martinez. I studied the passport photo. In it, he looked much younger than his 36 years and somewhat similar to me. Maybe with some dark contact lenses hiding my blue eyes and a bit of fake tan I could pass for this man. So I packed the documents too, in case I wanted to alter them for use as a false identity at a later date. With Europe's open borders, passports were not a pressing concern for me. It was about seven o'clock in the morning when I was done so I settled in for the day on his comfortable couch and switched on his laptop and TV. *Oh internet! How I've missed you!*

***

At eight o'clock I heard a key in the door. Alarmed, I jumped up and ran silently into the bedroom. *Who the hell is this?* I held the bedroom door open a crack so I could see into the hallway through the narrow gap. A middle-aged lady entered and put her bag on the hall table. She closed the door and looked at the packed suitcases I'd left by the front door with a puzzled expression.

'Monsieur Martinez?' She called out.

Damn. A cleaning lady! I rushed into the hallway, placed my hand over her mouth before she had a chance to scream and bit her neck. I drank about a pint and then wrestled her to the floor and held her mouth and nose shut until she lost consciousness. I went to the kitchen and got a sharp pointed knife and disguised my bite marks with some stab wounds watching jealously as the puddle of blood under her head grew. Then I stepped over her and moved the suitcases out of harm's way. It wasn't what I'd expected, but it might fit nicely into my plans. Juan Martinez had just killed his cleaning lady, taken the money in her purse and the small gold necklace she always wore, then packed his best clothes and valuables and fled in his car. I was sure the police would go with that and

118

not suspect a vampire at work.

I settled back on the couch with the laptop and was surfing away to my heart's content, when I heard a mobile ringing. I dashed around looking for the thing and found it in the kitchen. I picked up and said hello in French.

'Juan, where the hell are you?' came back a male voice in Spanish.

I made my voice all croaky and replied in Spanish, 'I'm ill. I'm not going to be able to make it in today.'

'But Mr Hardwick is coming over from London, especially for this meeting at eleven,' the voice said desperately.

I glanced quickly at the phone screen which told me that a certain Enrique was calling.

'I can't! I'm covered in red marks, it may be measles or rubella; it could be contagious Enrique!' I said hoarsely, trying to sound near death's door. 'You'll have to take the meeting for me.'

'Me? Have you lost your mind? I'm your secretary! I'll ask Amanda if she can fill in.'

'Yes, of course. Yes. Ask Amanda. Tell her I'll owe her big time,' I agreed quickly.

'Ok, I'll call you later. Drink plenty of liquids.'

'I will. Thanks Enrique!' I said and hung up. *Blimey, this is all getting a smidgen too lively.* Getting back to my internet surfing and channel hopping, I was like a starved little kid suddenly let loose in a sweet shop. I had too much information and stimulation at my fingertips, and then I discovered Juan had some porn channels so the laptop got put on charge and some very entertaining nakedness got my full attention. At four in the afternoon Enrique called me back.

'How are you feeling, Juan?'

'Just awful Enrique, I don't think I'll be making it in

tomorrow,' I croaked. 'How was the meeting?'

'Amanda did great and Hardwick signed the contracts,' he answered, upbeat.

'Good. I'm pleased it turned out well,' I said, sounding fatigued.

'You sound in a bad way. Have you seen a doctor?' he asked me.

'I phoned him and he agreed it was probably measles and I should stay indoors. He doesn't want me coming into the surgery with a contagious disease. My cleaning lady got me enough food to last me for a few days.'

'Ok. Get well and I'll phone you if there are any problems.'

'Thanks Enrique. I'll call you tomorrow morning for an update.' I hung up and switched my attention back to some French maids who were getting up to all sorts with feather dusters.

***

Immediately after the sun had set over the horizon, I made preparations to leave. I liked the apartment, but sharing it with two dead bodies wasn't ideal. I also didn't want to bump into any more unexpected visitors. Rigor mortis had set in and Juan put up some resistance to being folded over, but I still managed to roll him in a quilt, take him down to the BMW and bundle him into its boot. No one watching would have suspected that the quilt wrapped over my arm contained a dead body, seeing the ease with which I carried it. Next came the two stuffed suitcases and the laptop and I was ready to go. I put Juan's phone and wallet in my pocket and set off.

I needed to dispose of the corpse so I set the GPS to go to Berlin, hoping I'd find a suitable location to dump it along the way. I remembered there were some marshy areas by the river Somme ideal for the disposal of unwanted bodies. When I had last been in the vicinity in 1944 or 45 it had been a quiet rural backwater and when I drove around the deserted narrow roads I saw that nothing much had changed. I drove on until I saw water and no farmhouses. I had wrapped the body in some black bin bags before rolling it up in the quilt and now I added a couple of Juan's heavy soapstone bookends to weigh it down. I threw the corpse as far out into the watery marsh as I could and it sank immediately. With any luck, it should sink further into the mud and stay down there undetected for many years to come.

The detour had cost me a lot of time and I realised I wouldn't make it to Germany before daybreak, let alone get right to Berlin. I reset the GPS to find a suitable roadside hotel where I could settle in for the day. Hopefully it would be a few days yet before the cleaning lady was found and pretending to be Juan became useless. I decided to check in with Enrique at ten o'clock to get the lie of the land and deflect suspicion for as long as possible.

'Morning Enrique,' I whispered, still sounding deathly.

'Not feeling much better then?' asked Enrique, obviously concerned.

'No, I didn't sleep well last night and I'm still running a fever. I'm afraid it's going to be a few days more.'

'Amanda seems to have things in hand here. You just get well and I'll call you if we need anything.'

I imagined this Amanda must have been relishing Juan's absence and was probably already smelling promotion. *Sooner than you think, Amanda!* 'Thanks Enrique,' I replied and hung up. I spent the rest of the day in the comfort and peace of my hotel room. I thought it best to start ditching evidence as I didn't want Juan's trail leading to Carl-Heinz's door. I crushed up the mobile and as soon as it got dark I set off, scattering small phone parts from the car window. I decided to ditch the car in Cologne as it was a big place and the police wouldn't have a clue where Juan had gone next. I went hunting for a replacement model in a different part of town and found an old beaten up BMW that I knew I could hotwire and wouldn't attract attention. It was another five hours to Berlin and I was very tempted to pay the delightful Emmy a visit, but I knew that'd be the first place they'd look for me so I played it safe and made another stop at a motorway hotel.

Chapter 15: Schatzi

I paid my hotel bill and set off as soon as it got dark. I had been incarcerated for close to six months and now I was enjoying every moment of my freedom. It was a beautiful, warm August night and I drove with the windows down to let the warm air blow through my hair. There were many things I wanted to do and a big city like Berlin would hide me and provide everything I craved. I also wanted to see Carl-Heinz: he, more than anyone, would understand what I had been through. I might have been spared the horrible experiments he'd suffered, but I'd found being locked up quite hard enough.

I arrived in Berlin at about three o'clock in the morning and parked the old BMW in a quiet, leafy suburb. I was hungry but not very hopeful of finding anything to eat this early in the morning so I decided to take a walk before hiding in the car boot until the next night. I was walking past some nice villas with large gardens and thinking there might be some rich pickings there when an urban fox appeared in front of me, probably attracted by its own version of the rich pickings provided by unsecured bins. We stared at each other for a moment, he deciding whether to run and me deciding whether I really wanted to try fox. Then he turned and tried to slip through a hedge, but not before I got hold of the tip of his bushy tail. I dragged the animal back through the hedge as it yelped, in that eerie way foxes have. It tried to whip round and bite me but didn't even get close. The poor thing cried out in terror and I quickly grabbed its muzzle, silencing it while sinking my fangs into its neck. I'm not a fussy eater and I'm a firm believer in trying to bite into something at least once, but this animal had such a curious taste it wasn't something I'd be in a great hurry to try again. But blood was blood and it would keep the hunger at bay for a while longer.

I pushed the drained body under the hedge and continued my stroll, but something started to nag at me. Cats aren't eaten because they taste so vile. The Koreans and I agree that dogs are food, but people kill foxes for other reasons. *Nobody eats foxes. Why is that?* And then I had a vivid vision of myself running around foaming at the mouth and biting people. *Fuck! Rabies! I could have fucking rabies!* It was a prospect that scared me senseless. I'd read that it was a very unpleasant and painful way of dying.

Now utterly convinced I had rabies, I locked myself securely into the boot of the car. Hopefully my disease-deranged mind would forget how to get out again and the population of Berlin would be safe. I lay alone in the dark, feeling terrified and right sorry for myself and waiting for the madness to take hold.

And nothing happened. The little beast must have been healthy, but I swore never to eat fox again.

***

As soon as night fell again, I drove the car into a more built-up area and sat observing my surroundings. I was taking a leaf out of Carl-Heinz's book and hoping to see an old lady go by. An old dear might live alone and invite a nice young man like me in for a cup of tea. She might even divulge her pin code if I asked her nicely.

Before long I spotted an elderly woman in a pink coat with an adorable bichon frisé in tow. I followed her and slipped into her building before the front door closed. She was fiddling with the lock of her front door as I caught up with her.

'Who is this adorable creature?' I gushed in German, kneeling next to the dog. It put its paws on my leg and tried to lick my face.

'This is Schatzi and she is two years old today,' the old lady said with a friendly smile.

'How wonderful,' I cooed. 'It's nice to share a building with a beautiful dog like her.'

'You live here?' she asked, surprised. 'I had no idea any of my neighbours had moved.'

'I don't think she moved as such, but I do believe she is in a better place.' I guessed there were bound to be a few more older residents like her.

'Oh no! Was it Frau Niemann on the fifth? I haven't seen her for a number of days and she was looking so frail,' the lady said, looking close to tears.

'Oh I'm sorry. I did move into an apartment on the fifth,' I said getting up. 'Did you know her well?'

She had now opened her front door and she hesitated. It would be bad form to leave your friendly new neighbour on the landing with the front door open so invitingly.

'Very well. Too well, in fact. Would you like to come in for a coffee, Herr...?'

'Lindtman,' I said, holding out my hand. 'Otto Lindtman.'

'Frida Offenbach,' she replied and she shook my hand.

I reacted slightly to the name. It was the same as Emmy's, but I imagined only that it must be a common German name. We went inside and she gestured for me to take a seat before disappearing into another room to take her coat and hat off. She soon came back out dressed in a synthetic floral gown. I spotted that she had that strange bluish colour of perm that

125

only ladies of a certain age have. A young girl with that colour of hair would be described as an eccentric Goth, but when pensioners adopted it nobody batted an eyelid. I wondered briefly if I should dye my own hair; I was a criminal on the run after all. I watched Frau Offenbach go into the kitchen where I heard her make coffee. Schatzi had already jumped on to my lap and was trying to lick my face again. I gently fended her off and had a look around. It was a typical old lady's flat, with old-fashioned furniture that still looked like new because she'd looked after it. Every surface was protected with a little doily or an embroidered napkin and, not surprisingly, there was a scarily large number of knick-knacks.

The only thing that worried me were the modern photos on the walls – by the looks of it she had a few children and several grandchildren, so I didn't think I'd be able to take over her flat without someone noticing. I should have got up and left right there and then, but something Frau Offenbach had said intrigued me. I felt there was a good story to sniff out here. And it was just good to talk to a human being again, someone who thought I was nothing other than a friendly young neighbour.

'Did Frau Niemann have any family?' I asked, when she came out with the coffee.

'No... well, she had an estranged daughter. Poor Lotte, she didn't have an easy life.' She sighed as she handed me a cup with steam rising from it.

Now my curiosity was really tickled.

'You're probably too young to remember, but this quarter of Berlin used to be behind the wall,' she told me taking a seat.

'I am and I'm also not originally from Berlin,' I said, holding my cup of coffee and looking around for a way to get rid of the liquid. She gave me a way out when she suddenly jumped up and went back into the kitchen. I quickly poured the hot drink into a plant pot – it might kill it but I would be long gone by then. Frau Offenbach came back out holding a plate of some biscuits which she offered to me. I politely declined.

'So, have you and Frau Niemann lived here long?'

'We both moved in here in 1966, when we were newlyweds. In those days these were very desirable apartments and you only qualified for them if you worked for the government and were a party member. She went on to tell me that her husband, Horst, had worked as a border guard and Herr Niemann, or Stephan as she called him, had a job as a secretary in the ministry of internal affairs. Frau Niemann, or Lotte, and she had struck up a friendship when they discovered they were both expecting their first child. The two couples got on well and often spent the evenings in each others' company, the men enjoying a beer over a game of chess and the women swapping knitting patterns and helping each other out with making baby clothes. Sometimes the men had heated arguments if the conversation turned to politics. Stephan was growing ever more disillusioned with the party and had nothing good to say about his bosses, accusing them of being corrupt and short-sighted. Horst, on the other hand, loved his job and firmly believed he was keeping the capitalist pigs out rather than keeping his own countrymen in.

'You see, Herr Lindtman–'

'Call me Otto, please,' I interrupted.

She didn't offer me first name terms yet. Like the French, Germans stood on ceremony and used polite forms for as long as possible.

'You see, Otto, my generation was brought up after the war under communism. We were told that fascism was bad and

127

that communism had triumphed over evil. We were also spoon-fed propaganda about the decadent, corrupt West. I really didn't care about politics. I watched the wall go up but I was young and only cared about keeping a nice home and starting a family.'

'I don't blame you. I've never cared much for politics either,' I said.

'Horst was more idealistic and joined the party as soon as he could,' she said, and then went on to tell me how Horst's beliefs were soon shattered when he was out on patrol along the wall one night and someone tried to get to the western side. The man got up and over the first fence just a few meters in front of him. One of his colleagues took aim and shot the man before he reached the next obstacle. They'd all had their orders to shoot to kill, but they'd all hoped never to have to. Horst had to help recover the body from no-man's-land.

'I only saw my husband cry once, and that was the night he came home after this.'

'Terrible thing this wall must have been,' I commiserated.

It had got late and no matter how much I wanted to hear the rest of this story I had to make a move. I said my goodbyes and promised Frau Offenbach that I'd pop by again. Then I made my way to the fifth floor where I now knew an infirm, old, childless woman lived. I let myself into Lotte Niemann's apartment and found her already in bed. I switched on the lights and sat on the side of the bed. She just lay there staring at me, paralysed by fear. For a moment I thought she was already dead, but then I spotted her lip quivering. She had long, unkempt grey hair and was very frail. I could barely believe she and the spritely Frida were the same age.

'Be a dear and tell me your pin code,' I said smiling.

'5642,' she stuttered, eyes widening in terror.

I quickly put her out of her misery and then had a look around the flat. It was much like her friend Frida's but more modest. It looked as though she had fallen on hard times and there weren't many items dated after 1970. She didn't have any photos on the wall. *Great, this should be a good shelter for a while.* I'd never checked with Carl-Heinz about what he did with the bodies, so it wouldn't be easy for me to get rid of a corpse in the heart of Berlin. I took her keys and parcelled Lotte up in a few bin bags before carrying her to the car. I took her cast iron frying pan and some other heavy items to weigh her down, then I drove out of town and found a quiet stretch of the river Spree where I disposed of her. I wasn't sure what the calmly flowing river would do to the body, I just hoped I had attached enough weight to keep her down there for a while. I got back to the flat just before daybreak.

Chapter 16: Lotte

I spent the following day clearing out Lotte's personal things. All her clothes, knick-knacks and medicines went into bin bags. Then, finding an unsecured wifi network, I started to do some research. I had to find out if George was really dead and get in touch with Emmy. I discovered she was working for the local council in Paderborn and thought I'd best give her a call there as her home phone would probably be monitored. I had been locked up a long time and was pretty paranoid, so I wasn't at all sure that the work phone would be safe, *but would the Germans really let the French bug a local government phone?* I decided they wouldn't and dialled the number. The receptionist put me straight through when I asked for Emily Offenbach.

'Hi! It's Cameron here.'

'*Cameron!* Are you free? Did you get Dad's message?' she asked cheerfully.

'I assume you mean his obituary?'

'Yes. We told all our friends and family that the paper made a horrible mistake and luckily nothing else came of it. I mean, my Aunt Olivia was pretty upset and wanted to sue the paper but Dad managed to talk her out of it by saying it was a way of getting a message to somebody. My Aunt knows it's best not to ask her brother too many questions!'

'So where is he?' I asked.

'He's just about to go to Nigeria. He said the two of you were working on the job before things went pear-shaped.'

'That was ages ago! We never went ahead as the hostage was killed before we had a chance to go in,' I told her, puzzled.

'It's another hostage taken by the same terrorist group. Because he's already done the reconnaissance on the ground, he thinks he'll be able to move quickly and get the hostage out before anything happens.'

'He's going by himself?' I asked perplexed.

'No. He's going with Terry Porter, an ex-SAS colleague of his. I met him a few times and Dad assured me he's one of the best men he's ever worked with.'

'Ask him if he wants me to come along,' I said, hopefully.

'I don't think so, Cameron. They're leaving in a few days. I think they're all set.'

'Well, wish him luck if you speak to him before he goes,' I said, disappointed.

'I will. I'd like to talk longer, but my boss is giving me dirty looks. Can I take your number?' she asked suddenly.

I gave her the number that was written on the phone and told her not to use her own mobile if she called me back. I even asked her not to call me from her home in case the place was bugged, but I hoped she'd phone me soon. I really needed to talk to friendly human.

Night fell and I went looking for Carl-Heinz, stopping by all his favourite diners. I spent many hours waiting in front of various hospitals, but I didn't see him that night. I was cold and hungry when I made my way home. I stopped off at a cash dispenser to check how much Lotte had in her account and moaned out loud when the display indicated a balance of only 150 euros.

'Just enough for a decent bottle of champagne,' I said out loud.

'Mmm mmm mmm... champagne...' I heard a drunken, slurred voice behind me.

In Monaco, I would have invited the voice's owner straight

back to my yacht, plied her with champagne and sleeping pills and enjoyed a fine meal. Here I was living in some old biddy's drab apartment and the only thing in the fridge was a rancid packet of butter. It was all too depressing. I turned round, smiled at the girl, said 'Good for you, darling,' and walked away.

'Waaaait!' she shouted out after me, urgently.

I turned round and took a closer look at her. I'd expected a drunken teenager, but she seemed older and was quite smartly dressed, if a bit dishevelled.

'Look, I'm lost! I'm here for a conference and now I can't find my hotel.' *Oh dear. Normally straight-laced office manager gets to go away on a work jolly and misbehaves.*

'Which hotel are you staying at?' I asked.

She told me the name of a hotel that I had passed earlier and knew to be just a few streets away. I took her arm to steady her and promised I'd get her there. She prattled away in slurred sentences that didn't make too much sense, but I gathered she was from Dresden and was an account manager. She also kept going on and on about her cat. Which, bizarrely, she had named Clicquot after the brand of champagne. According to her he was the cutest cat in the world. I growled under my breath 'You'd better be tasty,' but she didn't notice and babbled on drunkenly. We got to the hotel and she gave the clerk her room number. Nobody batted an eyelid when I went upstairs with her. I took off her coat and shoes and laid her on the bed. She was asleep in a matter of minutes and didn't stir when my fangs opened up the vein in her leg. Seeing as she had bored me with her cat stories I sampled more than usual and took off all her jewellery, thrusting it in my pocket. She also had about a hundred euros in her purse. The poor woman would find herself robbed and hungover to hell the next day, but hopefully would have learned a valuable lesson.

I got back to the apartment just after daybreak having had to run the last few streets as the sun started to blister my neck and ears. *Note to self: go online and take note of sunrise times, you numpty! That was too close for comfort!*

***

The next evening I was looking fine and dandy again and thought I'd pay my neighbour, Frida Offenbach, another visit. I was eager for her to continue her story so I'd picked up a box of chocolates at a petrol station to woo her with. I rang her doorbell and Schatzi started barking. Soon the door opened and Frida opened it looking pleased to see me. I waited impatiently in my seat as she made coffee and put the chocolates in a china dish.

'I have a granddaughter of about your age,' she said as she handed me a cup.

'I work from home and am new to this city so I don't meet many nice girls. Does she live in Berlin?' I asked innocently.

'No, which is a shame, as I'd love her to go out with a nice young man like yourself.'

I smiled and shrugged my shoulders in a disappointed gesture. 'You were telling me before about the previous tenant of my flat, Lotte Niemann. So what happened to her?'

Frida took up the story where she had left off, telling me how her husband had been so shaken by the shooting of the escapee that he'd started to see the regime though more critical eyes. Conversations over the chess games became less heated as Horst and Stephan began to agree that East Germany had its flaws. Stephan confessed that he had thought of leaving. He wanted to take his young family to West Berlin to give his daughter a better life.

'How do you know that things will be better there?' Horst had asked frequently.

'I've not seen anyone coming over this damned wall from West Berlin. I think it's obvious that things are better over there!'

Horst wasn't convinced that uprooting the family and taking a dangerous trip to West Berlin was a good idea. He always told his wife that no regime that oppressed its people could last forever and he was certain things would change eventually.

'It took a long time though for that wall to come down.'

'Yes. We had to wait another 20 or so years before we could visit the West freely,' she said quietly. 'Nonetheless, my husband decided to help the Niemanns with their escape.'

Now I was on the edge of my chair. A daring escape over the Berlin wall! Just my sort of thing. I waited impatiently for her to continue.

'Of course, as a border guard Horst was ideally placed to identify the best place for escape. Construction of the Berlin Wall in concrete didn't start until 1965, so at this time it wasn't the reinforced wall we see the remnants of today. The biggest problem then was the space between the two fences that formed the separation between east and west. It was well lit with smooth, light-coloured sand that showed up everything and there were heavily-armed guards in towers with orders to shoot to kill. Horst picked a night when he wouldn't be on guard duty. The previous night, he had shot out one of the lights on one of the more thinly watched stretches with his boyhood catapult, knowing it would take a few days to be fixed.'

Stephan and Lotte were ready, she told me. Horst had told them where to make their escape and all the changeover times of the guards. They each had a small rucksack with some essentials and Stephan had the baby strapped snugly to his chest. They were both very nervous, desperately hoping that the baby wouldn't start crying. Fortunately, the Niemann's girl was a very quiet child anyway and a dash of brandy in her milk had put her soundly asleep. Lotte had been especially nervous, she'd later told Frida; she'd been shaking like a leaf and constantly gnawing at her fingernails. They'd waited until Stephan saw through his binoculars that the watch on the towers was changing, then the Niemanns had climbed quickly over the first fence with a small ladder and a heavy blanket to cover the barbed wire. They'd started towards the other side when suddenly the searchlight had come on and the young couple was trapped in a fierce light beam. Stephan had run to the last fence with the baby, blanket and the ladder and was straddled on the top before he even looked back. And there Lotte stood immobilised, like a startled rabbit in headlights, her hands raised and tears streaming down her face. A shot rang out and Stephan disappeared off the wall and into West Berlin never to see his wife again. Lotte had fallen to her knees and waited until the guards led her back to the eastern side and arrested her as a traitor.

'So Stephan and the baby made it safely to the other side?' I asked with baited breath.

'It took us a while to find out that the shot had missed him and that he and the baby were fine. First Lotte got a postcard from West Berlin saying that he and the baby were safe. Post was censored, so it was some time before a friend managed to get a letter across with the whole story. By then, Stephan had already found a job and an apartment and was settling into a new life in the West.

'In those days they loved us Ossies coming over and a helping hand was readily extended. Now they think we're a burden,' she added somewhat bitterly, hinting that not all was rosy in unified Germany.

'He didn't come back to be with his wife?' I asked, already knowing the answer.

'You have to understand that people who tried to escape were treated as traitors. He didn't really have a choice.'

'And Lotte?'

'Republikflucht was a serious crime in those days and could cost you three years in prison. I think they were more lenient on her as she'd already lost her daughter and husband, but she still served eight months,' explained Frida. 'Her sister moved into the apartment and kept the rent up, but she had to pull a few strings so that Lotte could keep the apartment. She visited her sister in prison as often as she could and helped her get back on her feet once she came out, but Lotte was a broken woman. We tried to help out as much as possible, of course, but we couldn't be seen to be fraternising with a traitor.'

'Horst must have had a few anxious moments. I mean, wasn't he a suspect just by living in the same building?'

'He was questioned and we worried that Lotte might give him up, but to our relief she didn't. And yes, the suspicion stayed and Horst never made any further promotion. I'm certain our phone was bugged and our mail opened, but we were careful and Stephan never wrote to us directly, so they couldn't prove anything.'

I had many more questions and wanted to know what had happened to the Niemann father and daughter, but I saw it was getting late so I brushed Schatzi gently off my lap and got up to leave.

'Come by any time you want to, Cameron. I hope I didn't depress you too much with my sad story. I do enjoy visitors. I don't get out much now that I'm a pensioner. My husband died four years ago, so it's nice to have some male company now and then.' She gave my arm a playful nudge.

'I certainly will, Frau Offenbach. I like to hear about the history of a place, even if it is tragic.' With that, I left for a nightclub to go hunting, but with only a 100 euros in my pocket it was going to have to be a cheap vodka marinade for my prey. I went to the type of club I normally hate and where they would have laughed me out of the place if I'd asked for champagne. I preferred fine dining, but I settled for a fast food cheeseburger in a mini skirt.

Chapter 17: Betina

The next day, a Saturday, Emmy called. She assured me she was alone and was outside on a new mobile. She hadn't seen any suspicious people in her neighbourhood or noticed anything out of place in her apartment, though she agreed it was best to remain cautious.

'Where are you staying, Cameron?' she asked me.

'I'm in Berlin, trying to find my friend Carl-Heinz.'

'I've got a granny in Berlin. I was thinking of paying her a visit. I could come and help you get back on your feet if you want.'

Now this was just too much of a coincidence. I told her about the Frida Offenbach in my building and asked if she and Emmy's granny where one and the same.

'That's her!' she cried out, amazed. Then added, more hesitantly, 'Is Schatzi still alive?'

'Of course she is! Your granny adores me,' I gushed, 'and she has some great stories about East Berlin.'

'I might be able to get away next week. We can talk more then. I'll let you know when I'm coming.'

I could hear in her voice that she was anxious about her grandmother, but I assured her I wasn't a big bad wolf and she had nothing to worry about.

I was very excited about seeing Emmy again. During my incarceration I had convinced myself that we were made for each other and though she might not quite have realised it yet, I would convince her soon enough. From the attention I got in nightclubs I gathered that prison had not wholly disagreed with me and I was still as attractive as ever. Once I turned on the charm, Emmy would see things my way, no matter what vicious rumours George had spread about me. Emmy fell into the right age bracket to have grown up with the Hollywood myth that vampires are brooding, misunderstood tortured souls that need to be loved and that – god knows where they got this from – TV and film maidens moaned in barely contained pleasure when we bit their necks. *Maybe I should give that another try… maybe she'll be the one that lets me!*

***

A week later, Emmy called again and said that she'd managed to get time off and that her granny would be delighted to have her to stay for a few days. I paid Frida a visit that same night.

'My granddaughter from Paderborn is coming to stay,' she informed me, beaming, when we sat down, 'but she is bringing her dog and I'm worried that he and Schatzi won't get on.' *Baz is alive and well and coming too? Brilliant!*

'Don't worry, Frau Offenbach. Your granddaughter's dog can stay with me if the two don't get on,' I offered. 'And anytime you don't feel up to walking Schatzi at night, I'd be happy to take her.'

She reached over and squeezed my hand. 'I wish there were more young men like you around. I do so hope my granddaughter agrees to a night out with you.'

I smiled my agreement and we talked about the news and other odds and ends for a while before I asked her to continue with her story.

'Lotte Niemann had it very hard, despite her sister's and our help,' she explained and went on to tell me that Lotte had been a secretary before her marriage, but with her criminal record could only find low-paid jobs such as cleaning or factory work. Letters from her husband were infrequent – it wasn't easy to find trusted people to carry them over the border to avoid censorship – but through the photos Stephan sent her, Lotte watched her absent daughter, Betina, grow up. The photos had shown an apparently happy, healthy child with blonde curly hair, but after Betina's fifth birthday the letters stopped altogether for a year. Eventually, Lotte had received a letter from Stephan explaining the silence. He had met another woman and wanted to get married again. He had sent Lotte divorce papers and urged her to sign them, as he thought Betina needed a new mother and his fiancée was kind and got on well with the little girl.

'She must have been devastated! Was there really no hope of her getting to the West?' I asked.

'She tried to get a visa, but she was an obvious flight risk so it got refused every time. She agreed to the divorce and asked her husband to keep sending her photos.'

'That is so sad. Tell me, did she ever get to see her daughter again?'

'When the wall came down in 1989, they met up for the first time since they'd parted. Betina was in her early 20s and had no idea who this woman was. It turned out Stephan had never talked much about Lotte; he must have felt some embarrassment about leaving her behind and by this time he had died.'

'What happened to him?' I asked. 'He can't have been very old in 1989?'

'No, he was only 45 when he died in a car crash in 1985.'

She sat quietly for a moment, still saddened by the tragic lives of her friends. She told me that Betina had continued to write to her mother after her dad had died and that when they were finally able to, they met up about once a year. However, Betina considered her father's second wife to be her actual mother and she and Lotte never really developed a close relationship. 'It must be Betina who is sub-letting the flat out to you. None of my neighbours seem to know either what happened to Lotte or that the flat was available for rent.'

'I rented through an agency,' I replied vaguely.

'Strange that no one told me Lotte had died. Betina must have known we were close once. Lotte had become very withdrawn and didn't talk to many people after she received the divorce papers but still, I find it strange that nobody knew. Betina and I met, so I would have expected a letter or something,' she said and I could see she was beginning to get quite upset.

'Maybe she isn't dead. Perhaps Betina just moved her mother into a home,' I suggested, 'and Frau Niemann told her daughter she'd said her goodbyes.' I didn't want Frida writing to this Betina.

She didn't look convinced and, getting uncomfortable with the direction the conversation was taking, I got up to leave mumbling something about a report due tomorrow.

'Let me know when your granddaughter gets here. I would love to meet her,' I said as I was leaving.

Emmy coming to Berlin was great news but things were otherwise bleak. I was getting nowhere with my search for Carl-Heinz and I started to fear that he'd moved on. Also autumn was approaching and winter in Berlin was certainly not a prospect I relished. I saw online that temperatures in December averaged between -3 and 2 degrees centigrade; far too cold for my liking. At some point I would have to move south again. Money and food was scarce. Bloody credit cards! Nobody carried cash around in their wallets these days. *Not to speak of responsible dog ownership! Don't people kick their dogs out at night to take themselves for a walk any more?*

***

About a week later there was a knock at my door. It was three o'clock in the afternoon and I had the curtains firmly shut. I quickly messed up my hair before opening the door. Appearing to be half asleep might explain the darkness in the apartment. I needn't have worried as there before me stood Emmy, all blonde and healthy and as beautiful as I remembered. She smelled alarmingly good as she wafted past me on her way in.

'Just about to go to my granny's, but thought I'd say hello to you first,' she said dragging a very reluctant Baz over the doorstep. 'I'm not going to let him bite you!' she tried to reassure the dog – in vain. He ran and hid behind the sofa as soon as she let go of his leash.

'I'm glad you are free and well,' she said turning to me and giving me a warm hug. *Boy she smells nice!*

'I don't think I have anything in the house to offer you. I don't entertain much these days,' I said apologetically.

'I'm not stopping long. Just wanted to see you were alright.' She looked around the apartment with some amazement; it was a very long way from the luxury of my yacht in Monaco.

'I think the previous old tenant died here, so I'm renting it cheaply,' I explained.

'Yes, old Mrs Niemann lived here. She was the same age as my granny, but she looked about a hundred,' Emmy said gaily, wandering around the flat. 'Anyway. I think Gran has already planned a date for us. Shall we pretend we don't know each other?' she asked, grabbing Baz's leash and attempting to coax him out from behind the sofa.

'Why not? Let's let the old dear play matchmaker,' I agreed, and opened the door. Baz darted out pulling Emmy out on to the landing at high speed.

'See you soon!' she yelled, as the dog dragged her away.

That evening, Frau Offenbach called to inform me that her granddaughter had arrived and ask if I wanted to take her out sometime. I actually felt quite nervous as, dressed in my smartest jeans and shirt, I rang the doorbell the next night. Juan had had some excellent stuff that I was now putting to good use and I'd even bought some flowers from the local petrol station. I don't think people do that much any more, but I could see Frida was impressed by the bunch of carnations. To my dismay, I saw Schatzi and Baz curled up together in a dog basket; the two were obviously getting along disappointingly well. Baz woke up and growled when he spotted me but stayed where he was. Schatzi, on the other hand, was very pleased to see me and kept jumping up and barked excitedly.

'Otto Lindtman,' I introduced myself to Emmy.

'Otto? You don't look like an Otto,' she said shaking my hand. 'Never liked the name Otto. I think I'll call you Cameron instead.'

'Fine,' I said, while her grandmother shook her head disapprovingly. 'I think I can live with Cameron.'

I took her to a trendy tapas bar in the centre. With all the wee dishes laid out between us nobody would notice she was the only one eating and drinking. She talked about her job, which sounded to me like a right snooze fest – something in urban planning – but she looked adorable trying to explain it all. We found that we had a shared love of football and sports in general. She told me she played football every Saturday and had considered making it a career, but her mother persuaded her to concentrate on her schoolwork and keep it as a hobby.

'It's very unfair. The men's game is so much better paid – I don't think there are many rich female players out there. But anyway, I think my mother was probably right and I do love my current job,' she said obviously resigned.

'So what are your plans, Cameron,' she asked and she leaned in towards me, putting her hand on mine.

I suddenly felt as nervous as a little boy; that unexpected touch, the concerned warmth in her voice. *She is seeing me with new eyes!*

'I really appreciated what you did for Dad, Cameron. If there is anything you need...' and she squeezed my hand. I took her soft hand in mine and looked deep into her eyes.

'Thanks Emmy, it's enough that you are here,' I said and gently pushed a lock of her golden hair behind her ear with my other hand. 'I've been thinking about you a lot. In fact, the thought of seeing you again really kept me going.'

I could see my melodramatics and the Rioja were having their effect as she cast her eyes downwards, smiling bashfully. She was unsteady on her feet as we made our way out of the restaurant – she'd had the whole bottle of wine to herself and I don't think she was used to it. I was pleased to have an excuse to put my arm around her to keep her steady. Then, once outside, she let me kiss her. And it was heavenly.

When she pulled away she started poking my chest. 'Dad warned me about you! He said you'd try something like that.'

'Your dad exaggerates. You don't have anything to worry about,' I replied, pulling her close again.

'You don't want to sleep with me and then never call me?' she asked coquettishly, and looked up at me with glazed-over eyes.

'I'd call you so often you'd get quite sick of me,' I said, kissing her again.

'Dad told me if I was ever stupid enough to go near you,

never to let you give me any pills. He said you have a habit of drugging girls.'

'Nonsense! He was just being the protective dad. I have only good intentions towards you.' Then, feeling more mischievous I added, 'Plus I don't think you'd need drugging, the Rioja is doing the job just fine.'

'I'm clear as a bell!' she said, but her slurred speech suggested otherwise. She moved her arms around my neck and showed me that not all good girls listen to their dads.

We moved on eventually, arms around each other, and came to one of the bridges over the river. We stopped to look at the Spree below and suddenly a painful memory washed over me. I felt my chest tightening and I needed to get away from the place. *Am I wrong to try to start something with Emmy?*

'What's up with you all of a sudden?' she asked as I grabbed her hand and started dragging her towards the U-bahn.

'It's late. I should get you home before your gran gets worried,' I replied curtly.

'Cameron! I'm a grown woman. I can make my own decisions. Don't worry about dad or gran or anyone else.'

'I know you are, Emmy, but even so I'm not sure falling in love with you is the right thing to do.'

She looked shocked that I had mentioned the 'L' word on our first date and we spent the rest of the journey in silence. When we reached her grandmother's apartment she turned to me and said, 'I never guessed you'd be so serious, Cameron. Can we not just have some fun and see where it goes?' She held my hands and leaned drunkenly against her grandmother's door. She looked so beautiful with her red, alcohol-flushed cheeks that I couldn't do anything other than take her in my arms and kiss her again.

'Goodnight, Emmy,' I said at last, pulling away.

'If my dad could only see you now, being the perfect gentleman.'

I smiled wryly and walked away. I was hungry, anxious and very confused. A good dinner would sort me out so I turned on my heels and headed for a nightclub. I went into a gay bar and let a 50-year-old take me home. I had already put a sleeping tablet in his drink before we left so by the time we got to his place he was already half gone and I had to help him open the door. When I sat him on his couch he closed his eyes and fell sound asleep. By the time I got home, I was well fed, 300 euros and a smart phone richer and feeling *much* better. I had convinced myself once more that things would be easier this time. Emmy already knew what I was and still wanted to be with me. *As she said herself, she is a grown woman with her eyes wide open. Where's the harm?*

Chapter 18: Helmut

Emmy came up the next morning to check I was ok. She had told her gran that she was going out to meet a friend.

'I had a wonderful evening. I hope you did too,' she said, wrapping her arms around my waist and looking up at me dreamily.

From that moment on, I was quite lost. All thoughts of wrong or right were forgotten and Emmy's poor grandmother was neglected as we spent all the time we could together. Frau Offenbach would have been mortified if she'd ever found out what unspeakable things that nice Herr Lindtman was doing to her little Emily upstairs. Four blissful days later, though, it had to end. Emmy had to go back to work and I had to figure out what I wanted to do next.

The first night after she left, I was depressed. It was only the end of August, but it had been a cold dreich day. I'd had the heating on since I arrived, but now it had stopped working. I hadn't paid the bills, so it had only been a matter of time before it was cut off. Needing some serious cheering up, I decided to push the boat out and go to one of the swankier bars. It would take my last bit of cash but, ever the optimist, I'd got by for this long and felt something would surely come along. I spotted two well-dressed 40-year-olds alone at the bar. I went up, introduced myself and asked the girls to share a bottle of champagne with me, but before I could place my order I had a familiar feeling that made my neck hairs stand on end. *Carl-Heinz!*

I looked around me to see where he was and had some trouble spotting him, but he soon found me. I barely recognised the sophisticated blond man in the Armani suit.

'Wow! You've changed,' I said impressed.

'You gave me a lot to think about after you left,' he said, shaking my hand. 'Am I interrupting something?'

'The ladies and I were just about to have a glass of champagne. Would you like to join us?' I offered.

'Don't mind if I do,' he said and confidently ordered a bottle of Moët from the barman. I was stunned when he handed over a 500 euro note from a large wad of cash. I was dying to find out what had happened to my maker but there was prey to be soaked and entertained first.

It was much later, at his apartment and after some more champagne and pills for the girls, that we had a chance to have dinner and catch up. I looked around the apartment with admiration. It was large and stylishly furnished. He told me he only used it to take prey back to, his actual accommodation and base of operations was in a different part of town. He suggested we go there and all would be revealed and having written a note for the two soundly asleep women he led me downstairs to his car. I was pleased he'd been such a good listener and had taken my advice in getting himself a nice BMW, but I was rather disappointed that we were leaving the nicer part of town behind us.

'You have to keep business and entertainment separate,' he explained as we stopped in front of a drab, high-rise building. The lift was out of order and the staircase was filthy. We climbed to the seventh floor where he led me into a small apartment. At first I didn't spot the little nerd with the greasy hair, as the place was so full of computers and other electronic equipment. Carl-Heinz introduced us. 'This is Helmut, my partner in crime.' Helmut's hand was warm and clammy and I couldn't believe Carl-Heinz would trust this, or any, human with whatever scheme he was involved in. *How on earth did these two meet? Does Helmut know?* Carl-Heinz only introduced me as an old friend who could be trusted.

The greasy-haired nerd soon crawled back behind his computer and Carl-Heinz led me into another room with a couple of comfortable chairs and a bookcase full of books. I saw a chessboard with an open book on chess strategy next to it and found it comforting that the man hadn't completely lost his old ways.

'So what are you up to? I barely recognised you,' I asked, eager to get some answers.

'After you left I had to admit to myself that I did want more comfort in my life. I'd grown tired of constantly moving and getting by. You saw the place I was living in at the time – a vampire surrounded by old ladies' knick-knacks and chintzy furniture. It was embarrassing,' he said, smiling ruefully.

Living, as I now was, in an old lady's flat, I held my tongue and let Carl-Heinz continue.

'I didn't have your confidence and natural flair, so I didn't really know where to start,' he looked rather sheepish at this point.

'So what did you do?' I urged him.

'I thought I'd try to make contact with humans when they are at their most vulnerable,' he said looking at his shoes.

'Which is…?' I urged again.

'I started going to support groups. Alcoholics Anonymous et cetera. I suddenly heard myself talking about totally made up problems and trying to pretend to humans that I was somebody else.'

'Good for you!' I said, amazed. I really was impressed, as I knew how awkward and reclusive he had been. I suppose the lure of capitalism had eventually got to even this Berliner.

Carl-Heinz had met Helmut at one of the meetings. He was

149

a computer whizz kid who had achieved a lot very young and couldn't cope with the pressure of what everyone then expected of him. He'd gone to study Computer Science at the Freie Universität in Berlin when he was only 15. As a young, impressionable teenager he'd started hanging out with other students amongst whom marijuana and hashish were commonplace. He soon learned that there were other drugs that could help him deal with the pressures he felt he was under. By the age of 18 he was a frequent drug user and things were spiralling out of control. His studies suffered and he began stealing from his parents to support his habit, which was how they discovered all was not well.

Helmut's parents found him a spot in rehab and by the time Carl-Heinz made his acquaintance he was 21, allegedly clean and trying to rebuild his life. The two of them attended regular AA meetings and Helmut had agreed to become Carl-Heinz's sponsor after he'd attended a few.

They began to meet outside the regular meeting times and as Carl-Heinz was an equally shy and nerdy, young ex-drug user, he gained Helmut's trust quickly. Carl-Heinz had fabricated a similar story about himself as a young medical student who had been led astray during his internship by the drugs so temptingly surrounding him. I smiled at that one, knowing the real temptation he faced in hospitals.

'Helmut's rather bitter about his parents having pushed him too hard and the university staff that didn't support him. We both feel we suffered at the hands of humanity and it's time to take something back,' he explained.

'Nice little criminal in the making there, then,' I said enthusiastically.

'Helmut is amazing! He can hack into any bank site and move money about without them noticing. We clear out the fake account before it's even discovered. I led Helmut to believe that I'd developed a spray that rendered me invisible on camera. It rationalises why I have no reflection, so that clearing out the cash can be my part.

'Do you need any help,' I asked keenly, the sound of a cash register ringing in my ears.

I saw Carl-Heinz hesitate and the old reserve was suddenly back. He might have admired me for my style and ability to gain wealth, but I was still far too lively and unpredictable for him.

I decided to help him out. 'It's ok.' I reassured him. 'I don't intend to stay long in Berlin.'

'I do hope you can stay a few days at least and enjoy a few more champagne dinners. You were not wrong there, Cameron,' he said shyly.

So the next day I packed up my belongings at Frau Niemann's and that night I moved into Carl-Heinz's fancy apartment. He didn't seem keen to have me near his business operations and I was happier staying in the nice place anyway. Before I left, I'd told Frida that my work was moving me to another location and that I wouldn't be coming back. I promised her I would write to both her and Emmy, but we both knew that was a lie – she knew that only the younger Offenbach would hear from me again.

That night, at Carl-Heinz's apartment, we talked about my adventures and he grew more anxious by the minute. He had known I'd been thinking of turning myself in, but he'd had no idea I'd spent six months locked up by the French secret service. Owing to his own experience of incarceration, he asked me a lot of frankly paranoid questions about being drugged or hypnotised.

'Are you sure they aren't following you? Maybe they're just

waiting to draw another vampire out,' he fretted. 'They might have put a tracker in you.'

'I don't think so. They didn't think I'd be going anywhere and I'm very careful in my communications with Emmy,' I assured him, but I could feel that Carl-Heinz now wanted me to leave sooner rather than later. I tried to steer the conversation back to him and the considerable risks he was running.

'Does this Helmut know you're a vampire?' I asked.

'Don't think so. We work together in the daytime and then go our separate ways at night.'

'He never opens the curtains?'

'He's not a big fan of sunlight himself, but I told him that the invisibility chemicals also make me light sensitive.' I raised my eyebrows at that one so he added, 'I'm a former medical student. I'm rarely questioned on such things.'

'What does Helmut do with his money?'

'As I said, he's bitter about a lot of things. I think he's putting it towards some elaborate revenge plot.'

I wasn't very happy with that answer. Nerds planning revenge might lead to a whole heap of trouble. My imagination started running away with images of Helmut building a doomsday machine. I daydreamed for a moment then asked, 'So you never ask Helmut what he gets up to in his spare time?'

Carl-Heinz looked uncomfortable as he thought about the strange situation he'd got himself into with this human.

'You didn't tell George everything. You said yourself that you knew nothing about his life. Helmut and I know as much about each other as we need to. We're both recovering drug addicts with secret, private lives.'

'What was Helmut's poison?' I asked. 'I bet it was coke,' I

said smugly. 'Are you sure he's not putting the money back up his nose again?'

Carl-Heinz began to show signs of irritation at this point.

'If you don't like it, leave,' he said tersely.

I thought it best to shut up then, as I rather liked the flat and the champagne-infused dinners Carl-Heinz was providing. I'd not seen myself in a mirror for many years, but in Carl-Heinz I saw a reflection of myself right in front of me: taller, blond but otherwise freakishly similar. I didn't like that I had created a clone one bit. When you're confronted with your own behaviour, you see your own faults far more clearly and all I could see was that we were nothing more than blood-sucking, callous parasites. I found myself missing Emmy's sweet face and, even more than that, her humanity.

I knew it was a dumb idea to visit her, but a couple of months had passed since my escape and I only intended to stay for a few days on my way down south. I stole an old car and packed up my belongings. I don't think Carl-Heinz was sorry to see me go, whatever he said. Vampires aren't meant to live together; all their petty jealousies and natural mistrust get in the way. He said I should visit again in the summer and gave me a nice wad of cash to help me on my way. With that, we parted company. I wasn't convinced I'd ever see him again.

Chapter 19: Terry

When I pitched up on Emmy's doorstep at about three o'clock in the morning, I found her in quite a state. Her eyes were red and puffed up and it looked like she'd been crying for hours.

'What on earth has happened, darling?' I said taking her in my arms.

It took a while for her sobbing to end and coherent speech to begin. My nice shirt had become rather wet with all the tears and what not, but I didn't have the heart to change it. I led her to the couch and held her hand as she composed herself. Apparently she had received a call from Terry who'd just come back from Nigeria.

Terry had got out the country with a bullet wound to the shoulder, but he hadn't been able to save her dad. He'd told Emmy that he and George were ambushed before they'd even reached the kidnappers' compound. Having pinpointed the location of the kidnappers' hideout and parked their Land Rover a mile away to continue on foot, they'd come under heavy fire as they approached the small cluster of huts amongst the trees and scrub. Terry had been shot in the shoulder and had seen George drop to the ground. He'd decided that the only thing to do was get the hell out of there and try and make it back to the Land Rover. He'd driven away at high speed not stopping to tend to his wound until he had put some distance between him and the gunmen. Bandaged up with the help of the first aid kit, he'd made it to the next town. It was a serious wound and he'd had to spend a few weeks in hospital before he was able to make his way back to Britain. He'd called Emmy as soon as he'd arrived, telling her he was sure that George had been killed instantaneously and that the kidnappers would just have buried him. Neither had had their real ID papers on them during the operation.

Emmy sobbed again quietly, holding her head against my chest, and my lips softly touched her neck. I smelled her blood and felt her body against me and a warm feeling welled up in me that then travelled downwards. I was getting aroused. I quickly pulled away. To make a move on her now would be utterly inappropriate and I'd ruin any chance I had of a relationship with her.

'Anything you need, you just tell me,' I told her.

'Thanks, Cameron,' she said drying her eyes and pulling away to go and wash her face. As she came back from the bathroom, she said, 'I need to get some sleep, I'm working tomorrow. Can you stay for a while?'

'Of course I can. As long as you want me to,' I said, kissing her good night. I wanted more, but it seemed neither the time nor the place.

When she'd gone to bed, I went over to rebuild bridges with Baz, but he wasn't having any of it and growled as I came near. I shrugged my shoulders and backed away. I had spotted a scrapyard with a feisty guard dog a few kilometres back and though I wasn't hungry yet I thought I'd pay it a visit the next day. I took Emmy's house keys, unloaded the car and had a look around the neighbourhood until it began to get light. I spotted nothing suspicious in the surrounding streets and didn't detect any bugs during a quick sweep of the electronic equipment in Emmy's apartment.

At seven o'clock, Emmy appeared looking hellish, but insisting on going into work anyway and leaving me by myself – totally by myself – she'd decided to take Baz with her and drop him off at a friend's for a few days.

I was nervous of being alone in her flat. I was paranoid about there being bugs hidden inside and agents waiting to recapture me outside. I had a good nose around the apartment, opening cupboards and drawers. Virtually every cupboard I opened greeted me with a shower of stuff that tumbled out on to the floor. *Gosh, the girl is messy!* I wondered if she had just popped everything into the cabinets in a hasty attempt to tidy up. The disorder made me even more restless – something had to be done. For me to feel at ease I had to create some order in the place so I found a bin bag in an overfull kitchen drawer and started to tidy, putting things she shouldn't have, or couldn't possibly need, in the bag. Snow globes, tacky holiday souvenirs and old catalogues – all went in. One by one, the cupboards and drawers started to take on a neat and organised appearance. She didn't realise it yet, but this girl really needed me in her life!

Once I was done with the living room. I stood at the front door and observed the layout of the apartment. The Feng Shui of the place was all wrong. I moved some furniture around and the room started to be more to my liking. I couldn't decorate, sadly as I'd need Emmy to buy me some paint, but I decided to make that our weekend project. I had no doubt she would be ever so pleased with what I had done.

I was, however, not quite finished. Now I had moved all the furniture around, the rug annoyed me. It was the wrong shape for the space, needed to be square and not rectangular. It took me no time to find some scissors in the neatly reorganised cupboards and solve the problem. Now I felt more relaxed! Nothing untoward had happened during the day and I waited impatiently for Emmy to come home. Hopefully, she'd be in the mood to pick up where we'd left off in Berlin.

When she finally did get home, she stopped short in the doorway and stood stock still for a moment before slowly walking into the apartment. I waited eagerly for her to sound her approval.

'What have you done?' she asked quietly. 'Why have you moved everything around?'

'It's a huge improvement, eh? The energy of this room was just all wrong,' I said, taking her arm and leading her around so she could admire my work from different angles.

'What's in those?' she asked cautiously, pointing at the row of bin bags.

'I tidied! Those are things you should have thrown away ages ago.'

She stared at me, her mouth slightly open, and looked from me to the bags. 'You decided to throw out *five* bags full of *my* things?' she asked, eventually.

'Isn't it all just so much more organised and calm now?' I was crestfallen. She didn't seem at all happy about the changes.

'The rug! Oh my god, you cut up my rug!' she cried suddenly, pointing at the floor.

'It was the wrong shape after I'd put the furniture in the right place,' I explained. 'Give it a few days! You'll find your apartment much improved–'

'Cameron! You can't just walk in here and throw out *my things* and move *my* furniture about!' She sighed heavily and then burst into tears. 'I can't cope with my father dying and then you destroying my home!'

I thought that a bit harsh, but she was obviously upset, so I decided not to quibble.

'I'm sorry, Emmy. I thought a tidy flat would make you feel better. It certainly makes *me* feel better!'

'Look, Cameron, I know you mean well. We'll just put everything back later,' she said drying her tears, 'It might at least take my mind off things.'

She went into the kitchen and made some dinner which she picked away at listlessly for a while before pushing it aside and heading for the bin bags. She went through them, pulling things back out.

'Cameron, honestly! This was a present from my grandmother, you can't throw this out,' she said pulling out a horrible porcelain knick-knack.

'It's hideous! The fact it came from your grandmother is no excuse to have poor taste on display,' I said, grimacing as the pink-skirted shepherdess was put back on a shelf.

'And Dad got me this!' she gasped her eyes flashing with fury. 'Never, *ever* touch my stuff again, Cameron. There will be consequences!' she warned grimly.

'I thought that might have been George's doing. I'm sure the man was colour blind,' I said as she lovingly placed a funny-coloured green vase back on the coffee table. Baz might just accidentally knock it over if he came back, then I could blame his tail for sweeping the monstrosity off the table and smashing it into many pieces. She finished with the bags and came to sit next to me, but we only talked for a short while before she called it an early night, exhausted from having slept so little the night before. It had been an epic fail on my part, but I was still sure that after a few days she'd thank me, once she got used to the new layout.

The next day, after she'd left for work, I carried on in the kitchen, throwing out food that was well past its sell-by date and giving the place a good scrub. There was dried up dog food on the cupboards and floor. The place was disgusting! Surely she couldn't object to a good tidy and clean when I had only thrown out rotten food!

It wasn't until I had my hand on the bedroom door handle that something stopped me. I realised I had already gone too far. Her wardrobe would have to wait, even though I was itching to start clearing it out. The shapeless pink Hello Kitty jumper she'd worn the previous night had no place in a grown-up woman's collection. I would bring her something stylish from one of my nightly outings – perhaps that would be the best way to start.

Time passed quickly and it was already three o'clock in the afternoon by the time I reached this decision. Emmy would be back in a few hours so I sat down to think. I couldn't imagine George being dead. I was sure the old rascal was trapped in some Nigerian village making a right nuisance of himself, walking around with a knotted handkerchief on his head complaining about the heat and picking fights with his captors at every opportunity. I was sure he would escape soon, call his daughter and say he was fine.

I had Emmy's heating fully turned up, but it was still too cold in her apartment for my liking and I found myself thinking about Rome again. I decided I would stay a few more days to console Emmy and then head south. Maybe over time I could convince her to follow me there, but if not I'd be back on her doorstep with the arrival of summer.

At about six o'clock I heard a key in the lock and Emmy came in, again by herself. I realised sadly that Baz wouldn't be living here while I was. She looked around suspiciously and without saying a word went into the bedroom. She came out a few minutes later and smiled. 'Sorry, Cameron. After yesterday's changes I feared the worst.'

'I didn't want to go in there without an invite,' I said, looking angelic.

'Stay out of there, Cameron! I mean it!' She started to sound upset again, but rallied herself. 'So, what *did* you do today?'

'I just tidied the kitchen a little,' I said meekly.

'Fucking hell, Cameron!' she shouted, heading straight for the kitchen.

'I cleaned too!' I said beating her to the kitchen door. I didn't understand why the girl was angry. I really had done her a huge favour.

Emmy stomped past me and threw open the fridge door.

'Where's all my food?' she cried.

'You could have killed yourself! There was loads of stuff well past its sell-by date.'

Emmy said nothing. She disappeared into the bedroom again, changed into jeans and a baggy t-shirt and then went back into the kitchen to make herself some dinner, complaining loudly that I'd left her hardly enough for a decent meal. I tried to start a conversation, but she just gave curt answers. After eating, she washed her dishes and then sat down across from me.

'What are we going to do with you?' she asked, hands on hips and looking like a parent facing a problem teenager.

I thought her look of pity was totally uncalled for, after all, *I* was here to help *her*. But before I could protest, the phone rang. It was her aunt Olivia. They discussed whether one of them should go to Nigeria and I felt powerless. There really wasn't much I could do apart from offer Emmy moral support and I didn't seem to be doing very well at that.

When she'd hung up, I tried some light banter to cheer her up. My charm offensive worked and we chatted for several hours. I really am great company and I had a ready stock of entertaining stories to distract her with. Emmy finally called it a night at 11 o'clock, telling me that despite going to bed early the previous night she hadn't slept much. I wished her a good night, took her keys and went out to find the guard dog I had spotted before. Sadly, if I was trying to seduce Emmy, I could hardly go to a nightclub and drag a drunk female back to the flat.

I got over the fence of the scrapyard easily and went hunting for the dog. The German shepherd was chained up near the front gate and it barked and pulled on its chain when it saw me. The barks became less loud and frequent as I came near and it bared its teeth hesitantly when I stood right in front of it. We had a brief tussle before I managed to sink my teeth into its neck. I didn't drink too much; I wasn't sure where my meals were going to come from, so thought it best to conserve the supply. Afterwards, the dog slunk behind some car tyres with its tail between its legs. The poor thing was chained up and would still be there for my next meal.

I could feel I had a lot of pent up energy so I took a long walk, exploring the neighbourhood to see what else there was to eat or steal. I came across a nice looking semi-detached with an empty driveway and after a quick look around spotted an open window at the back. I reached it easily via a drainpipe and hoisted myself inside. I found myself in the master bedroom, which suited me fine. I didn't want to cause a stir with burglaries in Emmy's neighbourhood, but I might get away with a few missing items if there was no sign of a break-in. The owner of the house looked to be roughly Emmy's size and had much nicer things, so I selected a nice Stella McCartney dress and was pleased to find the owner possessed a fabulous pair of Lamboutins that went with it. I rummaged around in some drawers to find accessories to complete the outfit.

I got back to Emmy's just before daybreak and had a

shower to make sure there weren't any blood spats or smudges showing. I hung the outfit up neatly in the living room and waited for Emmy to get up.

Chapter 20: Borussia

When she'd eaten her breakfast and was ready for work, Emmy sat down opposite me and warned me that I was not to go into her bedroom or touch any more of her stuff. There was a rather mysterious, Mona Lisa smile on her lips that gave me the impression she knew something I didn't. It made me uneasy, but I told myself that Emmy was a nice girl and I shouldn't worry. I promised her I wouldn't go into her bedroom – I was confident she'd invite me in soon enough. She got up to leave for the office, looking very sexy in her serious, dark grey suit with her hair pulled back in a sensible ponytail and I put my arms around her and told her she was beautiful. She looked pensive for a moment and was on the point of saying something when she spotted the outfit hanging up.

'Where on earth did that come from?' she asked, moving over to finger the fabric.

'Got you a present,' I said beaming. 'I thought we might replace the Hello Kitty jumper.'

I could see her anger building again at the implied criticism. 'And should I ask just where you went shopping last night?'

'I was astounded to discover that people hold car boot sales here at night,' I lied, unconvincingly. 'I hope you don't mind that it's second hand. I thought it would look lovely on you.'

She gave me a dark look and murmured something vague about being glad she'd done what she had. When I asked what she was on about she said she was running late for work and told me we'd chat later. I wished her a good day and she left.

I had my computer and Emmy had a few films on DVD that I hadn't seen, so I was hopeful that the day would pass quickly. As I sat down and switched on the computer I began to feel something amiss. My genitalia were suddenly feeling itchy. I mentally went over my last few sexual encounters, but I was always responsible, so I doubted I'd picked up any diseases. The discomfort grew quickly and I ran to the bathroom and ripped off my trousers and pants to discover I had a nasty rash all over my nether regions. *What the fuck?* I was baffled as to what could have caused it, and not a little alarmed. I gave things a thorough wash and had a look around Emmy's medicine cabinet to see if she had any lotion that might relieve the itching. The washing and just standing there pantless seemed to help and I eyed my discarded underwear with suspicion. *Is that what the mysterious smile was about?* I put Emmy's dressing gown on and gathered up all my clothes to put them through a hot wash. Three loads later, there were wet things strewn all over the flat to dry. Meanwhile, under the dressing gown, I let it all hang out and though the fresh air relieved the itching, the rash still hadn't completely cleared by the time I heard her keys in the door at six o'clock.

'Wash day, Cameron?' she asked, obviously amused, looking at all the drying clothes.

'You wouldn't know anything about that would you?' I asked grumpily.

'You touch my stuff, you never know who or what might touch yours,' she told me, smiling. 'You left some garlic behind in your great kitchen clear out...' And then she added, more seriously, 'And if you touch any of my neighbours' stuff, I might do worse.'

I was pissed off. I was supposed to be the big bad vampire,

164

there to sweep her off her feet and here I was sitting in her dressing gown with a smarting crotch. I grabbed some clothes that were nearly dry and disappeared into the bathroom. Her apologies failed to lift me out of my foul mood and I left the flat as soon as I could, heading out of town into more rural surroundings. If anyone had seen me they might also have spotted the dark thundercloud hovering above me. I was silently cursing Emmy, as the rash still bothered me, when I spotted a small pony in the back of a field. I looked around to see if there was anyone nearby and, when I verified that I was alone, raced towards the little horse where it bore the brunt of my anger.

When I felt full and calmer I looked back at the carnage. I'd made rather a mess. *Oh dear! This won't do at all. Emmy should not get wind of this!* The field wasn't far from some woodland near Altenbeken, and though I didn't think they'd had wolves in the area for the past century I wondered if I could make the wounds look as though a lost Russian wolf or a pack of feral dogs was responsible. It wasn't pleasant tearing up the flesh when I didn't feel like eating, but the end result was, in my opinion, rather damning for Mr Wolf.

My clothes were now a bloodied mess though, so I cleaned up as best I could at the horse's watering trough. The shirt was beyond help, so I dropped it in a dumpster on the way back to town. I made sure I stayed away from the apartment until the early morning to ensure that Emmy would be asleep when I got back. I showered and did another load of washing. She'd be none the wiser.

I made her some breakfast when I heard her moving around in her room and, when she emerged, I told her I was sorry and that I'd deserved what she'd dished out. I couldn't have her thinking I couldn't take a joke. I already felt rather silly and ashamed that I'd taken things so badly, and decided that I really needed to do a better job of keeping out-of-proportion vampire feelings in check around her.

'That's very big of you, Cameron. I hope you learned your lesson. And seriously, don't even *think* about robbing any more of my neighbours.'

I promised sincerely that I wouldn't. *How stupid would that be? If I'm going to burgle it won't be on my own doorstep!* I tried to explain that I'd felt nervous about being in the apartment, that I was worried that the DCRI was still after me and that I felt better when things were tidy and organised. She gave me a big hug and promised she would try to be tidy, as long as I didn't throw any more of her stuff out.

'But that is still a horrible vase and I'm not going to rest until you throw it away,' I said, only half joking.

'I'll put it somewhere else if it annoys you that much,' and she lifted the eyesore and took it into her bedroom.

I promised her I'd be on my best behaviour from then on, hoping that the pony wouldn't make the local papers, and she left for work looking more upbeat than she had for a while. I was very happy to see some of her former spark back.

I spent the day watching DVDs while I meticulously ironed all my freshly-laundered clothes – I do like to look smart, unlike Emmy who probably didn't even know she had an ironing board if her dishevelled look was anything to go by. I was sorely tempted to do her clothes too, but thought better of it. I had learned my lesson. Emmy came back at about six o'clock laden with supermarket bags and I eagerly helped her put the shopping away – I had rearranged all the cupboards in the kitchen and I didn't want her to mess them all up again.

'Now I understand why you and Dad were such good friends. He was infuriatingly neat and organised too,' she said, smiling ruefully. 'I still can't believe he's gone.'

'Must be an army thing. You have to be organised and methodical because your kit is so important; if you don't look after your gun, you die.' They had drilled that into us soldiers and somehow it had never left me. What she'd said about George and me was true; we'd had very similar habits which had made living together a lot easier.

'Shall I cook you something?' I asked, trying to impress her.

'You can cook?' she asked, pleasantly surprised.

I had often cooked for Hélène, as she tended not to look after herself when she was going through a bad patch. I couldn't taste it, of course, but she'd told me it wasn't bad. Emmy got changed while I whipped up a quick pasta dish with some of the ingredients she'd brought home.

'Not bad for someone who doesn't eat himself,' she said, smiling.

Halfway through dinner she started rooting through her bag and pulled out a newspaper. 'Guess what, Cameron, you're not the only supernatural thing in town,' she said unfolding the paper. With dread, I spotted a picture of a pony in a field. 'A poor little pony was torn to shreds during last night's full moon. They're talking about a werewolf attack.'

'Wow! I should be on my guard. According to myth, werewolves hate vampires!' I said, reading the paper with feigned concern.

'Probably just a big dog with rabies,' she said mockingly and took the paper off me to throw it in the bin. She didn't appear to have suspected me for a minute. She finished her dinner and I helped her clear away.

'I don't think he's dead,' I blurted suddenly.

'Who? The pony?' she asked, bemused. 'You think he'll come back to terrorise the neighbourhood like a were-horse?'

'Er, no. I was thinking about your dad.'

The smile left her face and she looked down at the cup she was drying absentmindedly. Then she turned to me and I could see hope that I might know something she didn't in her expression.

'What makes you say that? Do you know something or have some sort of sixth sense about him?'

'He's just tough, that's all,' I said quietly. I had no real reason to suspect he was still alive apart from a vague feeling and the fact that I knew George really well.

'I hope you're right,' she said looking deflated and I wished I'd kept my mouth shut.

'Aunt Olivia thinks we should have a service seeing as the British Embassy has heard nothing about any wounded hostages,' she sighed.

I pulled her on to my lap and tried to make her feel better in my own special way. Finally I got my longed for invitation to the bedroom, but I kept in mind that if I touched anything else but her in there, there'd be hell to pay.

***

My feeding still had to stay well hidden from Emmy. She had given herself to me willingly, but I knew I hadn't totally won her over yet. Fortunately, I'd discovered a farmhouse not too far off that I could reach in about 20 minutes at a steady jog, so donning some sports gear I told Emmy I was going for a run, to let off steam after being cooped up all day.

At the farm, I went to explore the large sheds I'd spotted behind the house. To my delight, I found they contained about 50 cows. *Ya beauty! I've hit the jackpot – this is food sorted the duration!* I fed to my heart's content and did the jog back about five minutes faster. Buoyed up by the food and exercise, I felt like waking Emmy up again, but I wasn't sure if she would find it romantic or irritating, so thought better of it. Instead, I decided to make her breakfast in bed and wake her up with a kiss just before her alarm was due to go off. I got the sweetest smile in return and I lay next to her to watch her eat. I didn't want her to leave for work, but she told me they had an important project they needed to finish by the end of the week so she had to go.

'What are your plans, Cameron? What will you do all day?' she asked me.

'I don't know... Perhaps I should start writing my memoires.'

'Hey! That's not a bad idea. Or maybe we could find you some work that you could do online. We could register in my name if you don't mind using my details.'

Hmm! Work! Not my favourite word in the dictionary.

'I just don't want you robbing my neighbours again,' she said, sternly.

'I'll take a look at what's out there,' I said, bringing the conversation to a swift end. I should have packed my bags and headed for Rome right then, but instead we ended up looking together to see if we could find some translating work that I could do easily. I studied the rates and decided it looked like a lot of work for very little pay. I could make way more in a single night by going back to my old trade. I knew Emmy still needed me, but though I had only been there a week I was bored. The September weather was too grim and cold for my liking and I was dreaming of warmer, drier climes. Since Emmy had decided to let Baz stay with a friend for the duration, unable to trust me alone with him during the day, I couldn't even get a daytime snack and in this cold I needed more frequent sustenance. I was well miffed with her about that. *He was my dog in the first place!*

The final straw came when I spotted a black van that I didn't like the look of in the neighbourhood. Something about it made me uneasy and I decided to break the news of my departure to Emmy the next day.

'I think I'll have to leave soon,' I started.

'Why? What's happened?' She looked stricken.

'Firstly, I'm not at ease here as they may still be looking for me, and secondly, it's getting colder here, which means I'm hungry all the time.' I looked down at my feet and went on. 'I might be putting you at risk.'

'You wouldn't harm me, would you?' she asked, shocked.

'I'm thinking of going to Rome,' I said, avoiding the question. 'I'd love you to come with me.'

'I can't just leave everything behind and live as a fugitive in Rome.'

'I thought you'd say that,' I sighed.

'Well, I at least need to think about it, Cameron. As much as I like you, I can't just up and leave. Do you need to leave immediately?'

I should have said yes, but I was still convinced that Emmy and I were meant to be together... and the sex was amazing. Perhaps if I stayed a little longer and gave her time to think and plan she'd realise she couldn't live without me either and come with me to Rome. So I decided to stay another week and we settled into a routine.

At the weekend, she said she wanted me to meet some of her friends. They were all wondering who the mystery man that had come into her life so suddenly was. Her football friends were a fun bunch of girls and I felt right at home amongst the hard drinking, sports-daft females. Emmy

170

thought I was getting a little too cosy with them, but was happy they all liked me and didn't suspect I was anything other than a normal bloke that knew his football.

Her work colleagues were quite a different crowd and frankly I was bored to tears by them. Gerhard, the wet dishtowel who was looking after Baz for Emmy, brought the dog along and shot me dirty looks all night. I asked Emmy if she had told him anything about my habits.

'Of course not!' she said, aghast.

'Why is that guy giving me dirty looks then?'

'We used to date. You're the first since our break-up,' she admitted, a little timidly.

I could live with that! I was amused that I was getting up this annoying man's nose and made a point of holding Emmy's hand and being very attentive to her. I was even polite enough to feign interest in their work conversations, despite being ready to burn the city council down just so they would have something else to talk about. Emmy was content with how letting Cameron mix with normal people had gone and said she wanted me to stay. I looked into her beautiful eyes and put off Rome for another week.

But things were becoming more difficult. The more time we spent together, the more I came to realise that Emmy was actually quite boring and ultra-normal. She had an unhealthy fascination with honest work and kept pushing me to find some for myself.

And then I started to become jealous of her outside life. I didn't like that she left me by myself every day to go to work, and Saturdays were even worse when she went off to play football with her mates. By the time she came back from her match all bruised and muddy I was in a right strop.

'I'm so bored!' I whined. 'It's alright for you, playing footie

171

in the park with your mates, but I'm stuck inside on my own all the time.'

'I can't help being human,' she said running a warm bath. 'Shall we go out tonight, do something together?' She had, by then, stripped off which put me in an altogether different mood. We were still in our honeymoon period from that point of view and couldn't keep our hands off each other, but serious cracks were starting to appear.

She bought me a ticket to a football match to cheer me up. It was a lovely gesture; I couldn't remember the last time I had seen a live match. It would probably have been Hibernian in 1913. She took me to see Borussia Dortmund which was a very different experience from my last match. The stadium was huge, with thousands of people in the seats and a pristine pitch floodlit like daylight, without the bad effects. I found it increasingly hard to concentrate on the game though, surrounded as I was by warm, drunk and excited football fans. I can't even remember who they played and who won, I was so distracted by all the pulsing human life around me. When we came out of the stadium, I kissed Emmy briefly and told her I had to go. Dumbstruck, she watched me skip away and leave her to find her own way home amongst the rowdy football fans.

I had targeted a group of young men who were already very drunk and I followed them to the nearest bar. Soon they could barely stand and began to make their way to their respective homes. I followed the one who was most unsteady on his feet and he slumped to the ground a few meters from the bar, overcome by the cold night air. I went over to him, playing the good Samaritan, but when I knew no one was looking I sank my fangs into his wrist. He barely noticed what was happening. It was an unusually cold night so I flagged down a passing taxi and poured the man into it. I had left enough in his wallet to pay for the fare.

I felt rather pleased with myself and calmly looked for a place to spend the day. I found a derelict building and tried to make myself as warm and comfortable as I could. The guy hadn't tasted particularly nice – beer is not my favourite flavouring – but his warm blood now flowed through me and I felt content. There really is nothing like human blood and I had craved it desperately.

Emmy could barely look at me when I came back the next evening. Knowing she'd be pissed off, I had bought her some flowers.

'I was thinking of calling the police,' she hissed.

'Oh, darling. I can take care of myself,' I said touched.

'To give you up, you bastard! I can't believe I just let you wander off to feed on some drunken football fans.'

'Fan, singular. And he'll be fine! Actually, without me he might have frozen to death. I put him in a taxi and everything!' I cried, genuinely outraged.

'Oh how noble of you, saving a man from average 10°C September temperatures!' she retorted sarcastically.

'See how the lack of human blood is affecting me? It felt like minus 10 to me. You have no idea just how cold I feel all the time,' I said, pleading for her understanding.

'What am I *doing*?' she groaned.

'My feeding on humans is not harmful at all,' I told her. I knew I was already on thin ice but I went on 'here – let me bite you and you'll see that there is nothing to it. I'm very restrained.'

She jumped up and away from me. 'That will *never* happen!'

We'd watched *True Blood* a few nights before and I

173

reminded her of when Sookie had let the vampire bite her. 'See if it was that Eric Nordman guy, you'd let him do it,' I whined jealously.

'No I would not! If you bite me, I become food. I don't want to be another of your prey conquests. If you loved me, you would not want to bite me.'

She was right, of course. She meant much more to me than that and I dearly wanted to prove it in a human way. I apologised to her and told her I would never ask her again. I felt a grand gesture was needed to demonstrate my commitment to her. The flowers obviously hadn't cut it so I persuaded her to come out for a nice meal with me. Despite being slender she could eat for Germany so my token plateful ended up empty too.

With Emmy smiling again, I felt happy. I was walking with a girl by my side and all our issues were forgotten for the moment. On our way home, I spotted a tattoo parlour and dragged her inside. I wasn't sure what would happen when the needle pierced the skin or whether the ink would take, but I decided to give it a try anyway. I had 'Emily' tattooed on my upper left arm and she thought it touching, but when I suggested putting Cameron on her lovely arse, she was less impressed. My tattoo looked nice, but it was a tad wussy so I had the guy do 'Scotland' with a wee Saltire on my other arm.

For a while after that I was on my best behaviour, being the charming companion I know so well how to be, but it wasn't long before cold, boredom and the lack of human blood made me restless again.

Chapter 21: Dr Okagbare

And so, one Tuesday night I decided to tell Emmy once and for all that I couldn't live with her any more. I had tried, but the leopard couldn't change his spots. She became worried every time I went out and I could almost see her wondering *What's he feeding on? Who's he robbing?*

I had just sat her down on the couch to break the news when the doorbell rang. She looked at me and asked if I was expecting anybody. It had been a while since I'd spotted the black van that had spooked me but I'd never quite put the fear of being tracked down out of my head. I was halfway to the bedroom to find a hiding place or an escape route when Emmy asked who it was through the intercom. Nobody answered, but the bell rang again and Emmy buzzed them in regardless. She opened the door, went out into the stairwell and hung over the railing to see who was coming up.

'DAD!'

Oh fuck! I hastily renewed my effort to find another way out of the apartment, but there was no choice but to face a no doubt very angry father. I hid in the kitchen and let the two have their moment. *Christ! He could've called! Why leave your daughter thinking you were dead!*

The two of them were, of course, very pleased to see each other and I waited nervously wondering how the hell I was going to explain my presence. Then Emmy came in the kitchen, said nothing, but fixed me with a questioning look.

'Trust me Emmy. He won't be pleased to see me here,' I whispered.

'Come on out, you big coward. I'll soften him up,' she said trying to drag me out.

'You got a visitor, Emmy?' asked George from the other room.

Oh bollocks! Can't stay hidden now. I let her lead me out into the living room, and there was George looking a lot thinner, older and bearded.

'What the *fuck* is *he* doing here?' spluttered George, getting to his feet.

'George! You're alive!' I said, keeping my distance.

'Cameron and I live together, Dad.' Emmy, beaming, wasted no time.

And at that point George's legs buckled and he fell back in his seat, looking pale underneath his dark tan. 'Noooo…!' he moaned, looking from her to me, distraught. His worst nightmare – and god knows he must have had a few bad ones – had come true.

I wasn't going to say anything. Best to let her do the talking and convince him I was a changed vampire, suddenly worthy of his daughter. I looked expectantly at her and she took the bait.

'Cameron has changed a lot, Dad. We've been together a couple of months now, and Dad, he is really trying.'

She was putting on a good show and I almost started to doubt that our relationship was on the rocks. She couldn't really tell him that I had moved in but that the relationship had big problems. *Huge problems!* She had to pretend he'd been wrong about me and that she hadn't made the biggest mistake of her life despite his warnings. No, there was nothing else she could have said to justify my living here.

'Noooo!' He moaned again, his shoulders slumped, head in hands.

'Dad! We're *happy!*'

I had come a tad closer and taken a seat next to Emmy and

she had taken my hand in support. George was now rocking back and forwards in his chair. His head came up and he stared at his daughter, eyebrows raised in appeal, clearly hoping it was all just a bad dream. Finally, he woke up to the horrible reality when he saw our clasped hands and before even I could react, he'd launched himself over the coffee table at me. He managed to get a blow right on target, and broke my nose before I could grab his fists and wrestle him back.

Once I had him pinned over the small table he calmed down quickly, knowing he couldn't win. I let him go and straightened my nose bone before it could heal into the wrong place. Emmy came to my aid with some tissues and I went into the bathroom to clean up. It may have been my own blood, but any glimpse of the red stuff puts me in a different mood, and that certainly wasn't what I wanted now. The situation called for calm, domesticated Cameron that lived with his human girlfriend.

When I came back out, the two of them were sitting on the couch, she holding both his hands and telling him over and over that she was alright and happy. I went to get them some drinks and snacks from the kitchen thinking some normal activity would help break the mood. When I went back in, I turned the conversation to him.

'So where have you been all this time, George? The poor girl here thought you were dead.'

'I thought I was going to die a few times, but here I am,' he said, glowering at me.

'What happened?' I insisted, desperately wanting to get him talking, so his mind wouldn't be on the unholy alliance he'd just discovered.

He relented, knowing that Emmy at least needed to know his story. He told us that Terry and he had indeed gone to

Nigeria to free a hostage. The preparations had gone well and they'd located the compound, but then George's story started to differ from Terry's. They had not been ambushed, but instead had located the compound, gone in under the cover of darkness and freed the hostage. They'd silently killed the single guard outside the hostage's hut and the three of them were making their way back to the Land Rover when someone spotted them. Shouts rang out raising the alarm and at that point things went very wrong. They came under heavy gunfire and Terry was shot in the shoulder, but George took a bullet in the chest. The hostage too was wounded. Terry and the injured man managed to get to the car, but it was too dangerous for Terry to go back and rescue George and he'd left him there for dead.

'Why didn't he tell us that? We could have looked for you if we'd thought there was a chance you were still alive,' said Emmy, very upset.

'Terry probably believed I would soon be dead, even if I'd survived the bullet wound. I certainly thought I was going to die. The canny bastard must have delivered the hostage to his family and claimed the reward. He obviously thought that by altering the story he'd be able to keep all the money himself,' said George with an ominous grimace. He went on to tell us about the victim, as Emmy was rather mystified as to why she hadn't heard anything in the media about a hostage rescue.

'It was a rich Nigerian businessman that had been kidnapped. His family asked me for help and the deal was that there would be a reward payment but no publicising the fact that it was two foreigners doing the rescuing. I wanted to get out of Nigeria and see my daughter as soon as I could. I thought I'd contact the family later to offer my condolences.' George's face turned grim. 'I'll make Terry cough up.'

'He'll be crapping his pants when he sees you!' I said gleefully.

George shot me another filthy look. Just the sound of my voice got his blood up – I could feel it and fled to the kitchen. When I came out with fresh drinks, George was telling Emmy how he had survived.

The militia that had captured him had an Oxford-educated doctor who specialised in emergency medicine. After studying and working in England, he had returned to Nigeria, but had grown disillusioned with its government. His two younger brothers had joined the militia and, half to keep an eye on his brothers and half to fight the government, he had joined their cause. It was George's incredible good luck that this man had treated him when he was captured. Without his skill George believed he would have died for certain. When he'd regained consciousness, it was obvious he was not Italian and that the papers he'd had on him were bogus.

'Why didn't you tell them who you were? Gran, Aunt Olivia and I could have raised a ransom?'

'I didn't want them to find out I had a military background. I mean, they sussed out I was English but they thought I was an oil worker,' he explained. 'I didn't want you to start getting a ransom together, blowing all your savings on me. I knew I'd get out of there.'

'Aww, Dad!' and she gave him a big hug, which I'm sure he would have enjoyed if I hadn't been there.

'So how did you escape?' I asked, keen to get to the part where George killed some baddies.

'They were frustrated that I wouldn't tell them who I was, so I ended up in Dr Okagbare's hands getting stitches quite a few times. Funny thing, his name was Cameron too,' he said smiling wryly.

'See, we're a charitable lot us Camerons!' I said trying to piggyback on his obvious fondness for the doctor.

'*He* didn't lick his fingers after treatment,' he said, giving me a menacing look. 'Anyway, the doctor and I became friends talking about England.'

'No doubt moaning about how you couldn't get a decent cup of tea in Nigeria.' I couldn't help falling back into my old bantering ways with George, but he was having none of it. He took another swipe at me, but this time I managed to get out of the way, and George fell forwards face-first into the cushions of the sofa opposite. The coffee table groaned under his weight.

'Cameron! Can you just go somewhere else so Dad and I can talk?' said my girlfriend, exasperated.

'What did I do?' I whined, playing the injured party.

They both looked up at me with expressions that made me exit sharpish. I wanted to hear the rest of the story and Emmy would no doubt leave out the gory details in the retelling, but I knew when I wasn't wanted so I went to see my cows.

I knew too that Emmy would probably ask George to stay and would make up the couch for him so I would have to amuse myself until I couldn't stay out any longer. I walked along with my hands in my pockets grumpily kicking things that found themselves near my feet and thinking about the truth of my relationship with Emmy. We'd been living together for two months and were getting on each other's nerves. I was moody, because that year's autumn had been so cold and wet and I wanted the heating on full blast all the time. When Emmy came home, she'd turn the heating down and tell me I was a wasteful baby that didn't care about the environment. I would sit on the couch wearing five jumpers, sulking childishly and complaining that unlike her I didn't have human blood to keep me warm.

She was still messy beyond belief and never threw anything out which led to blazing rows about the useless, tasteless crap she insisted on keeping. And to top it all, as Baz was now living permanently with a friend and I needed some company and the odd snack during the day, I had procured two lovely Yorkies without her permission.

'I thought we decided no dogs,' she'd said, when she saw what I had brought back to the house. I had contacted the breeder over the internet and was rather pleased with my two elegant pedigree dogs.

'We decided *you* wouldn't have your dog here. These darlings are mine and I will look after them,' I'd said determinedly, digging in my heels.

'Apart from buying them dog food and walking them when it's light,' she replied glumly. 'I promise you this Cameron, if either of them dies, I'm kicking you out.'

'I used to breed Yorkshires! I'm great at keeping them alive!'

Emmy had hated the Yorkies. She'd complained that they weren't really dogs. She missed Baz but couldn't bring herself to let him come home and these long-haired, yappy little dogs were no replacement. I refused to let her trim their fur as I thought their long, sweeping coats looked more attractive when they walked.

'A: they look like ridiculous lap dogs. People think I'm some gangster's moll going outside with these toys, and B: the bottom of their coats get all muddy,' she'd told me with disgust. 'You constantly need to brush them to prevent their fur from becoming knotted and somehow their hair always finds its way on to my work clothes.'

Pff! As if you care about appearance! I should point out that you have an ironing board one of these days. I had bitten my lip on that one. I walked the Yorkies at night, didn't mind cleaning up after the wee monsters and had no sense of smell left for anything but their lovely blood. I couldn't see her problem with them. Then one day, Emmy hadn't come back when I expected from taking them for their daytime walk and I'd been worried that something had happened. When the three of them had returned a few hours later, two of them looked bald and pathetic.

'You mutilated my dogs!' I'd cried aghast.

'They had a sensible trim, you drama queen!'

I'd been furious. I wasn't allowed to rob, to drink human blood or even to snack on my own dogs and now she was telling me I couldn't even have their fur the way I wanted! I was feeling truly hen-pecked and frustrated and had refused to talk to her for the rest of the day. In the past, she'd have taken pity on me and cajoled me into speaking to her again, but she was getting tired of my tantrums and strops.

When that night had came, I'd driven to Dortmund. It was only an hour away but had a population four times greater than Paderborn so I could misbehave and no one would tell Emmy the next day. I had some sleeping pills that were simply burning a hole in my pocket and discovered I hadn't lost my touch during my life of domesticity. It hadn't take me long to persuade an attractive blonde to take me home with her. But the human blood only made me want more. I had deluded myself into thinking I was in love and nothing else mattered, but I was still the same old creature; I still had an overpowering appetite for blood, money and sex. As much as I liked Emmy, she wasn't enough. Maybe if she had agreed to come to Rome, it could have worked out, but it had gradually dawned on me that I wasn't enough for her either. She put up with me because letting me go would lead me to worse behaviour. She'd convinced herself that staying with me was good for humanity and I think she was hanging on to a faint glimmer of hope that I could be reformed.

Now, to cap it all, George was back and wanting to plant a stake in my chest. I was busy trying to convince him that I was a changed man who wanted nothing more than to be good to his daughter, but it was a big sham. I knew it and Emmy knew it too, I could tell, but neither of us was ready to admit it to the other. I was back to being a big coward and I didn't want to give George the satisfaction of being right about me.

***

George staying at Emmy's made things extremely difficult. At night I got kicked out as George couldn't stand the sight of me and kept taking swipes when I was in range. One morning when he was cooking up some bacon and I wandered into the kitchen, he stabbed me with a fork. He left it there sitting in my upper arm. It healed quickly but my shirt was ruined. After his breakfast, George ventured out, not wanting to be in the flat with me.

When the weekend arrived, his desire to be away from me gave me and Emmy what I thought would be some much needed bedroom time. In spite of the tensions, I was still very attracted to her physically.

'Why does your father need to keep staying here? It's been five days?' I moaned when we were alone the first Saturday. Emmy had been to her football training that morning and had came back tired and aching. She wouldn't let me in the shower with her and fended off all my advances. I felt unloved and unwanted.

'He's my dad. I can't ask him to go to a hotel. Maybe *you* should.'

I could tell she was in fighting mood and wouldn't be willing to give in to my demands.

'But I live here now too. Do I not get a say?'

'Do you live here? Even before Dad came back, I barely saw you in the evenings,' she said shooting me a suspicious look. 'I have no idea where you go and what you get up to.'

'I need to feed! I have to go further afield as I can't go and feed on the same cows every night,' I lied, feigning outrage.

'I smell smoke and women's perfume on you' she said accusingly. 'You can't live without human blood can you?'

Shit, she's sussed me! 'I do smoke occasionally, but I'm not sure where you get the perfume from,' I replied, lying my face off. 'I'm doing just fine on animal blood – trust me, there's only you.' I gave her one of my butter wouldn't melt looks and I saw her expression softening.

I tried again to get close to her and this time she let me. We had a great time and by the time George returned, we were playing happy couple again, Emmy lying all snuggly in my arms on the couch. I could see the disgust on his face, but his daughter was an adult and apart from sticking the occasional fork or knife in me, there wasn't much he could do.

We began to wear him down and he was starting to tolerate me. When we were alone together on the Monday, I asked him what he was planning to do about Terry.

'I'm going to see another mate of mine, Dave, in England. I discussed the mission with both him and Terry but Dave couldn't go in the end, so Terry and I did the job by ourselves. I think I'll take Dave to confront Terry. I have no doubt he'll cough up when he sees I'm alive.'

'You don't want me to help out? Rough him up a bit?'

'No, thank you. I don't want any more *help* from you!'

We sat in silence for several minutes.

'Do you really love my daughter?' he asked me suddenly.

'Yes,' I said, and I did – I just found living with her too difficult and stifling.

'What sort of future do you envisage for the two of you?' he asked, looking defeated.

'I dunno. It's only been a few months,' I spotted a glimmer of hope in his eyes at this remark so I added chirpily, 'Maybe a gothic midnight wedding!'

And, joy of joys, George picked up his ghastly vase which Emmy had hastily put back out on display when George had arrived and threw it at me! I ducked out of its way just in time and I heard it smash behind me.

'Only joking, George! She'd never get married without your blessing. By the way, I'm glad you broke that monstrosity, I've been trying to get rid of it for months but, as it was from you, she wouldn't part with it.'

'I've never been good at buying presents.' The slightest of smiles hovered on his lips.

'Well I'm great at it! Wouldn't I be just the ideal son-in-law!' I twittered on, trying to make the smile break right out, but I'd miscalculated again. 'Aww, come on, George. You used to be able to take a joke!' I said hastily when I saw him looking around for another object to throw at me. To defuse the situation I added 'Tell me how you got out of Nigeria.'

When I'd made him a cup of tea, George calmed down, settled into his chair and picked up the story. He told me that he had mostly been kept tied up and under armed guard. At first he'd chiefly been worried that it was only a matter of time before someone identified him from the pictures the militia had sent to all the oil companies. Then tragedy struck for Dr

Okagbare. The two brothers he'd followed so he could protect them were killed in a gunfight. One was killed outright, but the other died on the operating table despite the doctor's frantic efforts to save him. He was distraught and a couple of days later had made arrangements to travel back to Lagos to inform his parents of the loss of their two youngest sons. A Range Rover was prepared with provisions for the long journey south. The day before he was to leave, the doctor had come to say goodbye to George and as soon as the guard was out of earshot told George to get ready to move fast that night.

'Did you two shoot your way out of the camp?' I said, eager for some bloodshed and mayhem.

'No, the doctor wasn't going to kill his own kind, you nutter!' said George impatiently. 'He used some tranquilisers on the guards and then we made a hasty but quiet exit.

'So why didn't you call Emmy as soon as you got out?'

'Thought the girl would like to see her dad was still alive with her own eyes.'

We sat quietly for a while, and then I asked him what his longer term plans were.

'I have some money put aside and, assuming Terry pays me, I should be able to retire,' he told me. Then, smiling evilly, he added, 'Maybe I'll get a flat here in Paderborn to keep a close eye on my daughter.'

'You're not old enough to retire,' I said outraged. 'What are you, 40, 42?'

'I'm 44 and getting too old to get shot at. I'm not as quick as I used to be.'

'Nonsense! It just went pear-shaped because you didn't have me along on the job. Come on, George. I've been itching to go on another adventure!'

'I thought you were happy playing house here with

Emmy?' And there was that evil smile again. George knew me better than anyone and that is why he would love to have hurt me permanently if he could.

'I am!' I insisted, back-pedalling furiously. 'But Emmy wants me to earn money legally and our hostage business was always so much fun – and lucrative!' I wasn't going to let on that there was trouble in paradise.

'Cut the crap Cameron. You're bored out of your tiny, little vampire mind!'

Thankfully, Emmy came back from work at that point and I didn't have to deal with George's observation. During their dinner George announced he was going back to England in a few days and I was relieved. I could break up with Emmy without her dad standing over me. Emmy was only 24, she would bounce back in no time, even though no man would ever compare favourably with me. But that would be his problem. The mood in the apartment was better all round that evening and I was able to stay until both of them wanted to go to sleep.

Chapter 22: Otto

I went out to my cows with a spring in my step that night, making plans in my head for my return to Rome. I had taken the Yorkies along for the walk, but they couldn't keep pace with me so I ended up carrying them most of the way. I got a very strange look from a cyclist who found himself on the same deserted country road at midnight and realised more than ever that I needed to leave. Paderborn might not be a village, but I was noticeably out of place, and getting noticed was never a good thing for a vampire on the run. I needed to be in a large city that could hide me and keep me safe. I'd been an idiot to stay as long as I had, deluding myself that I could make Emmy happy and that anything other than blood would make me content.

It was about four o'clock in the morning when I and two very tired Yorkies headed back to the apartment to find George's bags packed and ready for him to leave. He got up early to say goodbye to Emmy before she went to work and once she'd gone, I tried to mend some fences with George. We'd been friends for a very long time and I had been a prat and was sorry for it.

'Don't worry George, I'll be gone soon too,' I said as he was about to leave.

He didn't seem surprised. 'I'm glad to hear it. The two of you really don't have a future,' he said, with a piercing look.

'She's a wonderful girl, I just wish I was less of a vampire.'

'You are what you are,' he sighed. 'Somebody should plant a stake in you, but even though you defiled my daughter I don't have the heart to do it. Just promise me you'll do the right thing and let Emmy be.'

'I will, George,' I promised.

With that, we shook hands and I felt I hadn't totally ruined things with George.

The next day I finally had the chat with Emmy. She too seemed more relieved than upset that I had decided to end things and move south. I knew she'd miss me in the bedroom, but that would be more than offset by the promise of getting her nice, boring, normal life back.

That night I went to great lengths to make sure she would indeed miss me, and that the next guy would have an impossible task coming close to matching me. It was a great night and we agreed to stay friends and keep in touch if we could, but the next day I packed and was ready to leave as soon as darkness fell. I was gone as soon as the sun went below the horizon and before she even came back from work.

***

Ah! Bella Roma! It is good to be in the south again. I'd been in Rome before and it felt like greeting an old friend. The Colosseum, lit up in all its splendour, the Forum and all the other fantastic landmarks welcomed me to my new home. In October, Rome wasn't exactly tropical but it was certainly warmer than Germany. My bones stopped aching and I felt more like my old self. To me Rome was a feast for the eyes and the nose. Italians smelled delicious and I had sampled many over the years.

My previous visit to Rome had been in 2007 on a holiday with Roberto, the young chap George and I had rescued from his kidnappers in Colombia at the behest of his wealthy father. During the rescue, we'd had to tell Roberto that I was a vampire. We'd had a long trek together back through the jungle, so keeping it secret would have been hard. He'd been so impressed with us that he'd told his father he wanted to move to France to work for Mr Cameron, as he annoyingly called me, and to learn French.

When Roberto had first come to live with me on my yacht in France we'd got on pretty well and I'd decided to take him along on the Rome trip. Normally George travelled with me if I wanted to go anywhere, but I wanted to see a painting exhibition and have some fun and I thought Roberto would be better suited as a holiday wingman. So we'd gone without George and tried to bond as two young guys determined to live it up in the fancy nightclubs. It had been great for a while, as Roberto threw his father's cash about liberally and there'd been no shortage of available signorinas. Roberto and I had had separate bedrooms so, despite knowing the basics, he hadn't yet had to witness my more sinister side.

After about three weeks of the high life, we'd returned to Cannes as George was keen to get on with the job that eventually led us to Afghanistan and meeting Rashid. Slowly, understanding of what I was and the reality about how I survived had begun to sink in and Roberto and I never managed to have a holiday like that again.

I knew my Roman accent was spot on, so I wasted no time in integrating myself into Rome's thriving underworld, first by observing the local players, then by making friends with the important ones and picking fights with their enemies. I made sure that my fearlessness and skill with a knife didn't go unnoticed.

The city fitted me like a glove and I soon had cash, a place to live and some very smart new suits. I blended in well with the Romans as I had dark hair and dressed in the more flashy southern style: designer jeans, white shirt and a few items of jewellery. Gold looks awful on my pale skin and silver burns me, so I'd been delighted when steel and titanium pieces started to appear in jewellery boxes. In northern Europe my style got me a lot of male attention, but not every well-dressed, well-groomed male wearing jewellery is gay. In Italy, it got me the attention I did want and I quickly fell back into my old ways. I was careful not to form any emotional attachments to my conquests, better if they were just food – enjoyable, fun food, but nothing more!

With my ability to make friends easily, I built up some interesting contacts who supplied me with heroin and I wondered why I hadn't gone into the drugs business before. For the first few weeks they only sold me small quantities which I dealt at night from under a bridge. Gradually my new friends saw that I could handle myself, was honest, prompt with payments and didn't use myself, so they arranged a flat for me where I could process the heroin too. It was a dull, laborious task cutting the pure drugs with baking powder, weighing everything and parcelling it up in little sachets, but I didn't mind. I couldn't do much else during the day and measuring precisely and packaging neatly suited my OCD tendencies.

I sold the heroin from the apartment I was in – no one found hermetically sealed windows strange in this seedy part of town. In fact, I was sure I wasn't the first to use the flat for drug dealing as the neighbours never made eye-contact and avoided me if they could. I would have preferred to live in a nicer part of town, but here no one asked questions and the rent could be paid in cash.

I did it all in partnership with the local drug lord, Luciano Gattoni, who I didn't get to meet until a few months in. The heroin never went anywhere near this man, but he pulled all the strings from his Roman villa and knew exactly what was going on in his city. Gattoni wasn't your usual thug. He was smartly, though conservatively, dressed and looked like a regular, 45-year-old businessman. He'd built his empire up slowly and carefully but, like all drug lords, he had a mercilessly violent streak and all the other members within his organisation had a healthy respect for him. In the underworld only fear buys that sort of respect.

Word got back to Gattoni about my strict enforcement of payment and smart dealing and he asked to meet me. He had a nice villa on a hillside just north of Rome and though he knew I didn't use drugs, he was surprised when I arrived and refused the glass of fine Barolo wine he offered me. We talked and discovered we had a shared appreciation of art, though he preferred the old masters. I admired the craftsmanship on display, but told him I preferred abstract art. Gattoni told me I was boy and knew nothing; in time I would learn to appreciate real art. I nodded politely. He had a few Renaissance paintings and bronzes, which he proudly displayed in his ostentatious Roman-style villa. Gilded furniture and marble columns aren't my thing, but I liked the art he had and we talked at length about the Italian masters.

As time passed, Gattoni developed an appreciation for my cruel side and how I always managed to get junkies to pay up and I soon became one of his trusted lieutenants and then his main dealer. I stopped dealing from my apartment and employed a number of runners to deal the drugs at other locations. Woe betide any of them that stepped out of line! Things were going swimmingly. I had everything I wanted: money, a warm place to live and a large city with plenty of hiding places and hapless victims. I felt safe and happy and believed I'd be able to stay in Rome for a while.

One night, I arrived back at my apartment with a giddy brunette in tow. She'd got awfully merry on the fine champagne I had poured down her all night and I was looking forward to some merriment. As I came closer to my front door, my neck hairs stood on end. *Carl-Heinz? Had he finally decided to visit the eternal city?*

I didn't really trust it to be him, so I led my surprised date back down the stairs and put her in a taxi. Then I went back up and opened my front door with some trepidation. Inside, I found a man I had not met before, but immediately knew, sitting in my comfy chair. *Otto!* He got up and turned to me, and in a single glance I identified that his suit was tailor-made and that the watch on his wrist was an expensive Breguet. This man had exquisite and expensive taste. I realised I was intimidated by my older and possibly wiser brother.

'What's up, Bro?' I said lightly, indicating my recognition and trying to sound young and cool in opposition to his effortless sophistication.

A faint smile played around his mouth and he raised one questioning eyebrow. *Man, I wish I could do that!* One afternoon, and unable to practise in front of a mirror, I had annoyed George intensely by following him around asking him every five minutes if my left eyebrow was raised higher than the right one yet. In the end he told me it was, but I knew he was lying just to shut me up.

'Hello, Cameron,' Otto said, and he stuck out a well-manicured hand.

'Hey Otto. How's it hanging?' I immediately wanted the ground to swallow me up; I sounded like a complete arse.

'Very well, I suppose,' said Otto his green eyes twinkling

with barely concealed amusement.

'Why are you here?' I asked, finally managing to compose myself. I observed my brother with interest. He looked about my age and was only a few centimetres shorter. He had auburn hair and, like all vampires, very pale skin. I sat down, but remained on the edge of my seat intrigued, but watchful. I realised I actually knew very little about Otto and wondered how much he knew about me. Otto sat down too, making sure he hitched up his meticulously pressed trousers as he did. He leaned back and looked at me for a moment before speaking.

'You didn't think the French secret service would let you just walk away and carry on causing mayhem, did you?' he began.

I'd been right to be wary. 'You work for the French?'

'No. The CIA. We got wind of your arrest and subsequent escape and we decided to step in.'

I've been followed all this time? 'Why did you wait this long to arrest me again?' I asked with trepidation.

'It was about a month after you'd escaped that the French contacted us. They picked up on the strange murder of that cleaning woman by the Spaniard in Paris, but the trail went cold after Cologne and the Germans were sceptical to say the least,' he explained.

'And the CIA was less sceptical because they had you on their books,' I surmised. I was worried. I hadn't expected them to follow me as far as this. How long had they been on to me and what had made them come for me now?

Otto explained that they'd been called in to help on a far more pressing problem for the French than Cameron Blair. Nanette knew the authorities were on to her and in spite of the fact that she was aware they had her physical description, she was hell-bent on revenge. The first victim they found was

194

of course Karim. She had done nothing to disguise the vicious vampire attack that had left his body mutilated and drained of blood. A couple of other well-known criminals, including both of Karim's brothers who were active in prostitution, had then turned up in similar circumstances. The authorities called off the search for me and put all their resources into finding Nanette – a vampire that killed so openly was a matter of national security. They'd hushed up the exact details of the murders so as not to spread panic, then after about two weeks of mayhem in Marseille it had gone quiet.

'You knew Pierre Leblanc didn't you,' asked Otto.

'Knew? What happened to him?'

'Nanette turned up at his home in Paris one night determined to find out where you were.'

Normally I relish the gory details, but I had quite liked Pierre and I didn't particularly want to hear the details of his torture and death. Otto, however, enjoyed presenting the illustrated details. I felt a bit queasy and somehow responsible looking at the crime scene photos.

'This was when they reached out to us for help,' he explained putting the graphic pictures away. 'The French couldn't afford to lose any more agents and they felt out of their depth. They were relieved when I came to debrief them.'

'Relieved? I thought they'd be freaked out by another vampire darkening their doorway,' I said, somewhat piqued. I felt absurdly jealous that they'd treated Otto like a valued agent when I'd just been locked up and questioned.

'I think they were just relieved that the CIA believed them,' explained Otto.

'So, have you caught her?' I asked hopefully.

'I caught up with her in Berlin and she has been dealt with,' he told me briefly, looking a little uncomfortable.

Now I wanted the details, and the gorier the better, but Otto wasn't forthcoming. He told me further information was classified. I knew that to be total bullshit – my brother was hiding something from me – but I gave in and asked him how he'd found me. I quickly discovered that he was a very serious and totally inflexible agent. It unsettled me; it's not often I can't intimidate or charm someone.

'We decided to sit on George for a while. As a former associate we thought you might contact him. We found no trace of him at first and then after further inquiries learned that he'd gone missing in Nigeria. I switched tack and placed a surveillance team on his daughter's doorstep.'

'Ah!' I gasped, 'And the Germans were OK with this?'

'The CIA has a good working relationship with the Germans, but we told them it was counter-terrorism.'

'So when was this?' I asked, desperate to know how long they'd been watching me.

'About five months back. To our surprise we found not only George back from the dead, but also you getting rather cosy with Emily Offenbach. I asked the agents to hold off until I got there, but both you and George moved on before I arrived.'

They might have followed Nanette to Berlin, but I was pleased there was no hint of them knowing anything about Carl-Heinz.

'My team had installed some bugs in Miss Offenbach's apartment, so it wasn't very long before we picked up your trail in Rome. We know all about your recent activities. Unfortunately of course we couldn't tape all the information you blabbed to your girlfriend, but it steered us to all the right places were we were able to gather useful intelligence. The Italian police will be delighted with all the evidence we can now turn over to them, I believe they've been after Luciano Gattoni for a while,' he told me rather smugly.

'And what about me? Am I going to be handed over to the Italians?' I asked sombrely. I wasn't keen on the prospect of being put back in a cell.

'You will be allowed to live if you co-operate with us.'

'I don't think I'd make a very good witness in court,' I protested.

'No, neither do I, but we have other plans for you,' he said and I knew it was pointless to flee or protest. If my clever brother wanted me dead I'd be dust in minutes. 'We'd better leave. I'll fill you in on the way,' he told me.

'Hang on a minute, I need to pack and... and... what about the daylight?' It was all going too fast and I desperately needed to play for time. 'Don't tell me those clever boys at the CIA have found something to stop us burning up in the sun?'

'Yes, they have actually,' he said sarcastically. 'It's called a blacked-out van backed up to the front of the building. Get packing Cameron, I want to leave within half an hour.'

I wasn't ready to just up and leave; there were still too many questions

'Why is the CIA coming for me now? You've known about me since the 1920s.'

Looking furtive, Otto quickly placed his finger on his lips, advising me not to speak on the subject.

'I have no idea what you're talking about,' he said brusquely. 'Now get packing, all will be explained on the way.' He gave me a look that told me further discussion would be futile and I'd best do as I was told.

I asked him what I should do with the Yorkies. He just raised that one eyebrow again and said, 'Not my problem, but they are not coming with us.'

I went into my bedroom and Otto left me alone to sort out my things. I packed my bags and tried to forget that the dogs been so much more than just very tasty food as I drained one after the other. I swore I would never get friendly with anyone, or any meal, ever again. Nothing lasts forever, apart from us bloody vampires. Then I found myself holding Hélène's picture in my hands. Once upon a time, I would have done anything to keep it, but now I was happier to destroy it than let Otto get his manicured mitts on it and use it as leverage. It burned slowly, filling the room with acrid smoke.

'What the hell are you doing' asked Otto, rushing into the room.

'Just dealing with my last bit of baggage. I'm ready for you now.' I stamped out the last few smouldering embers on the tile floor, picked up my suitcases and headed for the front door.

As promised there was a van parked right in front of the doorway and we dashed inside suffering only minor burns. The doors were closed smartly behind us by two unknown agents and we moved off swiftly. I looked around and saw that the van was specially kitted out for Otto. It was set up with a couple of comfortable desk chairs that were secured to the floor and a computer workstation with some machines that I gathered were for monitoring sound, as there were headphones attached. I wondered how long they had been listening to me.

'What does the CIA have in store for me, Otto?'

He told me they had read the transcripts of my DCRI interviews with interest, but it was mainly my last few years living amongst the rich and influential that had saved me from the stake, or whatever was the preferred method used by the CIA to turn my kind into dust. They were particularly interested in my friendship with Andrei Klimov, who they suspected of arms dealing and having links to terrorist groups.

I had met Andrei on the Cannes party circuit. He was far wealthier than I had been and used to throw great parties on his yacht. We had a shared interest in art and I had helped him improve his collection. I knew very little about his business dealings, but had certainly had a feeling that not everything was above board.

'I doubt Andrei is going to fill me in on his arms deals if I suddenly come back from the dead after confessing to a murder,' I said.

'We're hoping to get one of our agents close to him. You know him better than anyone else in our organisation so you could tell us about his predilections and habits. You selected paintings for him, didn't you?'

'Yes, but he never told me about his business dealings,' I said, unconvinced.

'We just want you to be involved in the operation,' Otto told me decisively. 'Klimov is in Monaco just now and we want our agent to make contact with him at a gallery opening there.' He seemed very sure of his plan. I couldn't see it going anywhere, but the prospect of being in Monaco again was exciting. It probably wouldn't involve boats and parties, but I was sure I'd find a way to enjoy myself.

We drove for most of the day, stopping only to swap drivers or fill up with petrol. I was curious about Otto's life, but had already worked out that he was hiding some of the facts from his masters. Whispering, I asked whether we were still being monitored. He shook his head and I finally got to ask all the questions that were plaguing me.

'Who were you before you became a vampire? I gather they

got some death row inmates to turn into vampires and experiment on,' I started, angling for a dark revelation.

Otto didn't speak for a while and merely sized me up with his green eyes.

'I wasn't on death row. My misfortune was that no one was going to miss me.' He went on to tell me that he had grown up in an orphanage and that, though bright, had been offered few opportunities to better himself so found life outside the orphanage hard. He was only 21 when he met Professor Lindtman's cousin, Albert, in a bar. The two men had talked for a while and Otto told him he didn't have any family. Albert easily lured him back to the facility with the promise of a job and there he was led into a room with Carl-Heinz who pounced on him at Albert's command, turning him into a vampire.

'What did you do after you escaped from the facility?'

'First, I got as far away from Berlin as I could, surviving on farm animals and keeping out of the way, probably much like yourself.'

'I think that, like me, you were attracted by the bright lights of Paris. I could have sworn you looked in on me in the 1920s,' I probed again.

'It seemed like a good place to live for a vampire. The Metro and the catacombs and a city large enough to go about your business unnoticed.'

Finally! It had been him in Paris. 'So you did see me in the twenties! Why did you not make contact?' I asked him again.

'It was by pure chance that I came across you. I was walking along the banks of the Seine one night, when I got this strange sensation. In the facility, we could always sense each other so I knew that it was another vampire nearby. I looked over the wall and on the bank below I saw you and a ginger-haired woman. You were looking around you nervously, so I gathered that you were the vampire and could sense me too. I kept my distance and followed the two of you home. I was quite surprised that you left before daybreak to spend your days in the metro tunnels.'

'She didn't know I was a vampire,' I said quietly. *My god! He saw Hélène!*

'I followed you for a few days and I saw the woman not coming to any harm. And apart from the rat population no one else seemed to either.'

'That's debatable,' I said softly.

He looked at me questioningly for a moment, but I wasn't going to elaborate.

'The thing is, I led my employers to believe I was the only one of my kind, a freak experiment in a German facility. Firstly, I didn't want to panic them with the news that there were others out there. Secondly, I didn't want to become a vampire hunter. You seemed pretty harmless, so I let you be,' he explained.

'Did you come across any others?' I asked, intrigued, but he shook his head. I hadn't realised we were quite such a rare breed.

'I'm sure there are more, but I don't want to go looking for them, and apart from those in our bloodline, I can't sense any others,' said Otto. 'I was fascinated by your interviews with the DCRI. I had no idea Carl-Heinz was still out there. I last saw him before I fled the facility in 1909.'

'He has changed somewhat recently' I said sombrely.

I saw Otto looking at me again with his interrogating green eyes so I quickly went on, 'He's still pretty harmless. He's friendlier with humans now, shares a flat with a guy in Vienna I believe.'

I didn't want Otto prying any further. I didn't quite trust him, so the less he knew the better.

***

Otto told me he'd arrived in Paris in around 1910 and I could hear from his voice that it had been a good time for him. After the reconstruction of the centre of Paris by Baron Haussmann in the 1860s, Paris had become a magnet to the rich and famous. Just as I was in the 1920s, Otto felt himself drawn to the wealthy Americans that were then living in the city, but he wasn't after just money; he wanted influence and a role for himself in the modern world. He realised that the balance of world power was shifting and that the old colonial powers were on their way out. He was convinced that the new world power was on the other side of the ocean and he observed, read the papers and carefully made contacts.

When war broke out in 1914 he was already working for American intelligence and knew many of the influential people in pre-war Paris.

'They just trusted you? Did they know what you were?' I asked scarcely believing him.

'I did have the ear of their intelligence chief in Paris. He was shocked at first when I revealed myself, but he could see my potential and so he kept my nature hidden from all the other agents. In those days I always worked alone, carrying out his – well, let's just say unsanctioned – projects!'

He smiled, so I assumed there were some fond, blood-spattered memories.

In the run up to, and during, the war his perfect German proved to be invaluable, but they also let him run riot on the battlefield. His loyal service earned him a permanent job with intelligence after the war, and he was gradually introduced to more people.

'So what do you do exactly?' I asked.

'It used to be assassinations, getting in and out of places that have CCTV or detectors that don't register vampires and also a lot of translation work, but recently I've been given a more prominent role.' He smiled wryly. 'Thanks to you and Nanette, I've been promoted, though I never wanted it to be as head vampire hunter.'

'Does the President know about you?' I asked, amused. I had a vision of Barack Obama receiving the nuclear launch code and with it a wee memo saying, 'Oh, by the way Barack, we've got a vampire working for us. He's actually our longest serving employee. Is it OK if we give him a watch for his loyal long service?'

'The head of the CIA knows, I'm not sure the President does,' he told me, obviously wondering why I was so amused. I thought I'd better explain and see if I could raise a laugh from my serious brother.

'I was just wondering whether that lovely Breguet watch of yours was engraved "for 100 years loyal service, love Barack".'

'No,' he said, pulling the sleeve over his wrist, seeming embarrassed that I'd noted the brand. 'Watches and clothes are some of the few luxuries I allow myself.'

'Do they provide you with food?' I asked eagerly. I was feeling a bit peckish.

He opened a small fridge with a broad grin and handed me a bag of A positive.

'It's processed to prevent clotting, but it's not bad,' he told me. I got stuck in greedily and nodded in agreement.

He went on to tell me that they had opened a blood bank in

203

Paris in the 1930s. Most of the blood had been used as the donor intended, but some was transfused into Otto, especially when they discovered that his language skills came via the blood. They were keen to get donations from a wide variety of ethnic groups and he mentioned with great pride that at the last count he spoke 83 different languages and dialects.

'Can you get me some Estonian?' I asked. 'That's the only European language that has eluded me.'

'I'll see what I can do,' he promised.

We drove for a long time, but finally the van slowed down and started to descend downhill. The familiar smells of Monaco drifted into my nostrils. I felt I had come home after a long absence. Otto watched me with a bemused smile.

'What are you so happy about?' he asked.

'Can you not smell that? The money and champagne?' I said surprised.

'The smell of money and champagne makes you happy?'

'Oh, aye!'

We stopped in front of a modern high-rise building and as it was night I was at last able to stretch my legs. Otto didn't want me to stray too far as my being there had to be kept under wraps. I jealously looked at the lights of the boats moored in the harbour below and sighed deeply. We went into the building and took the lift to the 15th floor where my home was going to be for the next few weeks. *So close to all the fun, but unable to take part. Torture!* The two bedroom apartment was large and simply decorated. Of course the CIA wasn't going to waste money on fancy furnishings and trivia like a sea view, but it seemed to be comfortable enough and I had a room to myself. As in the van, there was a lot of recording and monitoring equipment set up. There was a video feed running from a camera trained on a yacht in the harbour. I didn't recognise the vessel so I asked Otto to fill me in.

Andrei had got married to Tatiana the previous summer and the CIA had learned she was now expecting their first child. To celebrate the wedding, Andrei had bought a new yacht, the 85m *Tolstoi*. It was moored here in Monaco.

During my absence, Andrei's wealth had grown and grown. In addition to the villa in St Paul, he now owned an impressive penthouse apartment here in Monaco which overlooked the Casino, and the gardens and fountains in front of it. He might even have been able to see his yacht in the port below from his terrace. Tatiana would no doubt be having a whale of a time throwing money around in the various upmarket boutiques. Any self-respecting shop here would have one or more Russian-speaking shop assistants on hand to deal with the Tatianas of this world and save them the trouble of learning a pesky language like French.

I settled in and Otto and I shared a bag of A positive for dinner. It was ok but I knew I'd grow sick of it after a while and want something fresh. I thought I might add a dash of champagne just for taste.

The first morning, I was introduced to agent Stacey Welch. She was a stunner with a very ample bosom and flowing blonde locks. She looked like a very curvaceous Farrah Fawcett, and like Farrah in *Charlie's Angels* this woman was highly trained and knew how to handle a gun. Needless to say, I developed an immediate crush. 'This is the agent we think is best suited to gain access to Andrei Klimov,' explained Otto.

I had to stop myself from falling on the floor laughing. They obviously didn't know Andrei's type.

'Don't get me wrong Stacey,' I said laughing 'you're a

beautiful woman and I'd shag you myself in a heartbeat, but Andrei wouldn't give you the time of day.'

'I'm an art historian and I speak fluent Russian,' she countered, looking hurt.

Otto's face looked like thunder. They'd obviously spent a lot of time on this operation already. Out of pity I offered them some help.

'It's just that he's partial to model-thin, Russian girls. And I don't think he's much interested in having meaningful conversations with them... Andrei wouldn't be stupid enough to involve a mistress in his business dealings.'

'So what would your solution be to get close to Andrei?' asked Otto.

'Dunno. Maybe Stacey and I could have a brainstorming session over a bottle of Cristal,' I suggested with faint hope.

Otto's face grew even darker. I wasn't sure I actually liked the guy. He seemed very committed to his work and I knew he wasn't being totally open and honest with me. If his masters decided I was no longer necessary he would no doubt eliminate me without a moment's hesitation. I'd so far failed to find a sense of humour or a lust for anything other than duty in the man. But Stacey I did like, so I pulled her down on the couch next to me.

'Tell me Stacey, how long have you been with the CIA?'

She flicked her hair back and told me seven years, I stopped listening as I spotted some tell-tale marks on her neck. Otto was not only her boss but also the jammy fucker that was getting his fangs into this princess. I looked up and saw him staring back at me with a look that showed smugness but also menace. If I got too close to his prey, I would be dust. I moved away involuntarily. *How has he got her to let him bite her?*

'I think Stacey and I will do the brainstorming,' said Otto

and he gestured for her to join him in the other room. *His bedroom!*

She got up and followed him obediently into the other room and I watched with envy as the door closed behind them. The professional solution would have been for all three of us to have discussed a strategy but Otto needed to prove a point: Stacey was his and he wanted to rub my nose in it. The noises coming from said bedroom soon became unbearable, but it was light and I had nowhere else to go. I switched on a laptop but they had not given me access to the internet yet, so apart from playing solitaire and creating a brightly coloured poster in Paint that declared 'Otto is a dick!' I couldn't do much else to distract myself. I had now firmly decided I did not like my brother.

And then I got worried. Otto needed me to help him and he knew I wouldn't do it voluntarily. He wasn't willing to share his prey with me, so what did he intend to use for persuasion? Would it be carrot or stick? A clever fellow like Otto wouldn't make an enemy out of me without a reason – he must have something else up his sleeve. After what seemed like hours, the noises stopped and a few minutes later Otto came out by himself. Stacey was probably recovering from blood loss and whatever other nastiness Otto had subjected her to

'So Cameron, any suggestions as to how we can get close to Andrei?' he asked, as if nothing had happened.

I wasn't in the mood to talk to my obnoxious brother, though, so I replied moodily. 'I just saved you guys a lot of time by telling you what Andrei doesn't like. How you decide to proceed from there is your job.'

'However,' he said, 'if you help us and it leads to Klimov's arrest, we'll let you go and you can live your life as you see fit.'

I found that hard to believe. They had no reason at all to keep such a promise. Who would complain about a broken promise to a vampire? I'd found out what their carrot was, but I was still curious about the stick.

'And if I don't?'

'Things will get unpleasant. We have ways of making your life a living hell: silver, garlic and a bit of sunbathing... any number of such things might be on the menu.' He smiled menacingly.

I thought about it for a moment and decided that for the time being it would be better to play along and get to know Otto, find out his strengths and weaknesses. After all I was back in Monaco, had a roof over my head and was getting fed. I could imagine worse places to be.

'OK,' I began, trying to sound thoughtful. 'Well, we could try and turn one of Tatiana's friends. Andrei may tell his wife things that she might confide in one of her girlfriends,' I suggested. I doubted it would lead to any useable intelligence, but it might just get me out of the apartment and into the arms of a champagne-guzzling woman.

Otto sat up interested and I went on to tell him about my history with Olga, Tatiana Klimova's best friend. She and I had shared a night together on my yacht a few years before and though I had never called her she'd still seemed smitten and was ready to forgive me when I'd bumped into her some time after. The girl might be willing to work for the CIA if I subjected her to some special Cameron treatment.

I could feel myself getting enthusiastic about my role as James Bond – he was Scottish after all and women were known to go weak at the knees just at the accent. We talked until nightfall about how best to approach Olga and what to tell her about my miraculous rise from the dead. Otto was pleased with my input and rewarded me with a trip to the beach. Before I left, Otto suddenly shot something into my neck with a small gun; the bastard had put a tracker device just under my skin! He told me that they'd always be able to find me now.

One of the agents drove me to San Remo where I could jog for several miles along the seafront and get some much needed exercise. I felt physically better afterwards, but now hated Otto with every fibre of my being.

***

When I came back, the apartment was buzzing with activity. Stacey was up and about with a fresh plaster on her neck and working with some surveillance equipment. Otto explained that they had found out Olga's address and had already installed a camera that provided a live feed of the entrance to her building. He told me I was to go round to Olga's the next night and I was shown how to put bugging devices in her apartment. I noticed that most of the agents were working to Otto's time schedule; working when he could be outside and going to sleep at sunrise. Stacey and Bethany, another female agent, were sharing a flat a few floors below and Chad and Steve, the two other male agents shared another not too far away. Andrei must be important if the CIA was willing to devote five agents to him.

When I was alone with Otto, he handed me his phone and told me I could call Emmy and talk to her for half an hour. We'd stayed in touch and I told Otto I didn't want her to worry if I suddenly stopped calling. It was great hearing her voice and she told me that both she and George were fine. He'd gone back to England and had convinced Terry to share the payout with him. Emmy was concentrating on work and catching up with friends. Baz was fine too, she said, and then she paused. She went on hesitantly to tell me she had rekindled her romance with Gerhard, the work colleague she had gone out with before me. By the sounds of things, their relationship was now getting serious and I felt a sharp pang of jealousy. Having met him and found him to be such a dullard I was angry that she felt able to replace *me* with *him*. I was also disappointed that she appeared to have got over me so quickly, but I had to brush all murderous thoughts from my mind. I had enough on my plate. Emmy would probably be happy enough with less-interesting-than-drying-paint Gerhard. They could buy a semi-detached and have their 2.4 children...

I took a deep breath and managed to chat away airily for a few minutes telling her only that I was no longer in Rome, but back in Monaco. I pretended everything was fine and I was keeping out of trouble. She wished me luck and we ended the call.

Fucking Gerhard! I hope he and Otto spontaneously combust!

Chapter 23: Olga

'Cameron! I thought you were dead!' Olga's mouth remained open in stunned amazement.

'Olga, darling! I just had to see you! Can I come in?'

She opened the door hesitantly and let me in, clearly not knowing what to say. I embraced the flabbergasted girl and squeezed her to me as if she was the dearest thing alive.

'Olga, I've missed you so much and longed to tell you why we couldn't be together! Things have been so complicated darling.' I gushed like a lovesick teenager. 'Things are still complicated, but I simply couldn't live without you any more!'

She hung, motionless, in my arms while I waited for her response. Nothing.

'Olga, I love you!' I whispered, pulling back to look deep into her eyes, my own baby blues misting up. *Christ I'm good!* And then I kissed her with such passion and fervour that her knees buckled and I had to hold her up. I let her catch her breath, only to pick her up and carry her into the bedroom. She still didn't know what to say, but she made no effort to stop me. When she finally did find her voice, it was to moan in ecstasy.

A while later, we lay contentedly in each other's arms. I was satisfied, as I'd kissed her so roughly that her lip had bled and she was happy because I'd paid her a lot more attention than on the previous occasion. She was surprised but definitely pleased to have this new and nicer Cameron in her bed.

'I thought you were *dead*,' she said, tracing an invisible line over my chest.

Olga and I now communicated in French and I found that her grasp of the language had greatly improved over the past few months. I'd never let on that I spoke fluent Russian; eavesdropping was way too much fun. 'I had to disappear. Some powerful people are after me,' I said trying to sound frightened. 'They framed me for a murder I didn't commit!'

'I knew you couldn't have murdered Yvette. I never believed that you were a killer,' she said naïvely.

'Promise me you won't tell anyone I'm alive. Not even Andrei!' I urged her, holding her gaze until she responded.

'I promise, Cameron.'

My experience with Emmy had taught me that I didn't need to be afraid any more. Young and caring Cameron was well and truly gone to the point where I doubted I was capable of falling in love any more. And if I could, it certainly wouldn't be with Olga, no matter how lovingly she now gazed into my eyes. I decided that she had rested enough to be ready for round two and, finding I wasn't wrong, I greatly enjoyed myself. Afterwards, she fell sound asleep, so I got up to place a few bugs around her apartment. She had decorated in a modern and minimalist style and I was surprised to find some of Andrei's artwork on her walls. I wasn't sure what to make of that, but I liked her surroundings well enough to feel that spending time there would not be a chore. Having left her a note saying I'd be back the next evening, and signing it with 'I love you. Cameron', I left Olga's apartment and got into to the black sedan the CIA had parked in the next street.

At the apartment, Otto was waiting to ask me how my miraculous return had gone down.

'Very well!' I answered, and before he could ask for details I asked, 'By the way. What are you CIA boys going to pay me? I'm doing some of my *best* work for you...'

He replied tersely, 'You're getting your life and freedom; it's about time *you* paid something back.'

I could see his point, but was smug in the knowledge that I'd grabbed a couple of bonuses. I'd managed to feed a little on fresh human blood and I knew that the next night *I* would be subjecting *him* to the bedroom noises.

***

Later that night, I had Otto to myself for a while. He still hadn't told me exactly what had happened to Nanette and I had to know. It would give me an idea of how ruthless Otto was and what fate might befall me if I stepped out of line. I also wanted some assurance that she was really dead.

'From what I gathered in the interviews and from the Spaniard's abandoned car, it seemed likely you were heading to Berlin. Nanette would have had the same information,' he told me.

'How did you find her? Could you sense her?'

Otto told me he'd set up surveillance of the red light district around the Kürfurstendamm and Potsdamer Strasse, thinking Nanette might pick her victims there amongst the pimps and other lowlifes. He also frequented the fancier wine bars that he knew would attract me. He'd been astounded to bump into Carl-Heinz there one night.

'What did you do to him?' I asked fearfully.

'Nothing. He co-operated fully. He told me you had been in Berlin but were now in Rome and I believed him. He obviously had no idea you had been living with Emily in Paderborn. As I said, I'm not interested in becoming a vampire hunter so, as long as you lot stay out of trouble, I won't tell my superiors about you. I did warn him to distance

213

himself from that Helmut guy though. I couldn't let a human committing fraud on that scale go unnoticed.'

I felt sorry for Carl-Heinz. He'd have to start all over again and it was my fault. He'd be cursing me for leading the CIA to his door, but I was happy he was still out there. I wondered if he'd stayed in Berlin or if he would step further into my shoes and start exploring the world.

Otto went on with his story. 'Soon after, my surveillance team picked up a woman that fitted Nanette's description and they discovered her hideout. We took no risks and were well prepared. I staked her myself.'

'She's definitely dead then?' I asked, keen to make absolutely sure.

'Yes.'

Providing proof of a vampire death is nigh on impossible and the picture of a neat heap of dust he showed me could have been anything. I just had to take Otto's word for it, and his word was something I had very little faith in.

***

The following night I went over to Olga's armed with a bottle of champagne and a sleeping pill. Whilst I fully intended to exhaust the girl utterly, a bite might still be enough to wake her up. *Best to be safe.* The donor blood kept me nourished but the last bag of AB positive had tasted a little odd – perhaps it had been in storage for a while and lost some of its freshness and flavour. The little taste of Olga had been good though, so I was looking forward to fully flavouring and savouring her. She opened the door dressed in a sexy, black negligée and almost dragged me inside. She was talking filthy in Russian as she hastily undressed me, not knowing I understood

214

everything she was saying. She took my amused smile as a sign that her unintelligible ramblings were perceived as sexy and she enthusiastically launched into some very graphic language that made even this vampire blush – but only for a moment.

The dirty talk was actually quite fun, especially when I pictured Otto listening in. Later on, I opened up the bottle of champagne, which Olga drank eagerly while I emptied my glass, unnoticed, into the ice bucket. I spun her a long, made-up, sob story about how I'd been set up and where I'd hidden for the last few months having faked my own death. Olga hung on my every word, believing every bit of it judging by the look on her face.

'I'm not proud of it Olga, but I have made my money through the international arms trade. It made me very rich but it also made me some very powerful enemies.'

'Are these men still after you?' she asked anxiously.

'If they knew I was alive, they would be. You could be in danger too, darling, if they ever found out.' I looked into her eyes, my eyes dripping concern, 'So *promise* me you won't tell anyone about us.'

She promised again and I kissed her. The mix of perceived danger, secrets and a gorgeous mysterious man had turned her head completely and I felt I could begin my mission.

'Andrei was my best friend here, and I fear he might be in danger too,' I proceeded.

'Andrei? Why?' she asked, startled.

'He never told me outright but I think he might be in the same business.'

'Andrei is in the arms trade? I thought he was in investments of some sort,' she said, genuinely surprised.

'I'm not sure even Tatiana knows exactly what he does, but

if he is involved he could be in serious danger!'

She looked suitably worried. She and Tatiana had been friends since childhood and even though I thought Tatiana was a moody, spoiled bitch, Olga cared for her a great deal. From what I heard next I gathered that the Klimovs had been quite generous to her. She told me she worked in a jeweller's shop in Monte-Carlo, near the Casino. She made enough for food and clothes, but the apartment belonged to Andrei and she was staying there rent-free so she could afford to live in Monaco. She told me she was even allowed to borrow some of his art as he had so much that he didn't have space to hang it all. She seemed unconvinced that her generous friend would be involved in anything so shady and I could see that she was thinking hard about what to do. I put my arm around her shoulders and drew her close.

'Don't worry too much, dear girl. Have a careful talk with Tatiana. If he is just in investments, as you say, then they have nothing to be concerned about.'

Olga was getting drowsy, as I had mixed the sleeping pill in with her champagne, and she soon fell asleep in my arms. As I'd expected, she was delicious and I quickly felt revived so I decided to give my chauffeur the slip and misbehave for a while. They had the tracking device on me, but they would hardly risk drawing attention by dragging me kicking and screaming out of the Casino, so I had a few hours of relaxing fun at the poker table and walked out a few hundred euros richer. I also managed, undetected, to steal a watch from a fellow gambler's wrist. An oil baron from one of the former Soviet republics, he didn't have a clue about how to play the game, but he did have impeccable taste in wrist wear. Otto had his gold Breguet watch, but I now had a platinum one!

When I came out of the Casino, there he was, waiting for

me. I could tell from his expression that I was in a whole heap of trouble.

'What the *fuck* do you think you're doing?' he snarled, as I got in the back of the car.

'Shouldn't hang around outside the Casino, Otto. Too many tourists with cameras,' I waggled my finger at him.

I got a crushing blow to the face for my trouble. I knew he could hit harder than any human, even George, and the force of the punch left me dazed.

'Don't *ever* do that again! You seem to have forgotten that we have ways of making your life a living hell! And while you work for us, you can't steal. What were you thinking?' he hissed and grabbing my wrist he took the watch off and handed it to Agent Chad, who dutifully reported it to the Casino.

I retreated huffily into the corner, my face still smarting. My older brother was a humourless bully and my hatred of him was growing in a way I hadn't imagined was possible.

***

Olga was soon quite evidently head over heels in love with me. Otto had allowed me to have a phone so she could call me, but they monitored our conversations. The whole operation saw the gooey messages that Olga was sending me on an almost hourly basis. Stacey helped with texting back as I got rather sick of it after a while. Having her as my Cyrano de Bergerac became a formidable weapon in my maintaining Olga's heart, but although she would have been more than willing to share anything she knew, Andrei wasn't telling her anything. She'd carefully broached the subject with Tatiana, but told me later it hadn't been a success.

Tatiana really knew nothing of Andrei's business dealings and when Olga had raised the question that he might be involved in the arms trade, she'd seemed genuinely shocked. She'd said she would talk to her husband, but I didn't hold out much hope that it would lead to anything other than Andrei becoming even more cautious.

Olga and I were in her apartment, discussing the meeting she'd had with Tatiana earlier that day, when suddenly my phone rang, startling me – only Olga called me on that number and she was sitting right beside me. I looked at my watch and saw that it was about 11 o'clock.

'Cameron! Get out of there fast,' Otto's voice said urgently when I picked up. 'Andrei is on his way!'

He must have spotted Andrei on the camera by the building's entrance so I knew I had only seconds before Andrei exited the lift on the third floor. I calmly put my phone away and stayed where I was.

'Wrong number,' I said to Olga.

A few seconds later the doorbell rang and I whispered to Olga that I would hide in the bedroom while she went to see who it was.

'What the fuck have you been saying to Tatiana?' I heard a very angry, male voice say in Russian.

'Andrei, I just...'

Olga's meek reply was cut short by Andrei's furious tirade. 'Why the hell are you telling my pregnant wife I'm an arms dealer? Have you lost your mind?' he shouted.

'I'm *sorry*. I was sure there was no truth in it. I know you're an honest business man!'

'What did you hear? Who is spreading these rumours about me?' he was still shouting.

'I saw it on a website when I googled your name.' *Clever*

girl! She got herself nicely out of that one.

Hopefully the CIA boys were listening in and would immediately be setting up a hoax site as all this was going on.

'Well stop spreading that rumour. Monaco is like a bloody village and it's not true!' he thundered.

'I've only spoken to Tatiana. I thought she should know that there are these rumours about you. But don't worry Andrei, I swear I won't mention it to anyone else.'

He seemed satisfied with Olga's responses and left shortly afterwards. Olga was shaken but not too upset. She had known Andrei a long time and knew him as little more than a fun-loving party animal. I wasn't too sure though. You don't acquire the kind of fortune he had by being nice and I knew he had some shady contacts. If Andrei ever found out what was really going on, I feared for Olga's safety.

'Maybe you should meet Andrei, let him know he could be in danger,' she said to me later.

'Let me think about that. We'll leave well alone for just now.'

I left not long after, as I wanted to make sure the agents were planting the alleged gossip. There were a few stories I could usefully add. There was a particular Ukrainian who I'd had an argument with a few years before in a club, probably over me pointing out that shell-suits were not suitable evening wear. I couldn't wait to say something about the corruption he was involved in with the national football federation as Ukraine had just lost an important match. Messing with a man like him from beyond the grave would be priceless! I caught up with Otto and eagerly got into his car to go back to headquarters.

Chapter 24: Stacey

We returned to the apartment and later that morning I found Stacey alone in the kitchen making herself a coffee. She'd put the radio on and was swaying her hips gently to some music. Before I knew it my hands were on those shapely hips. She leaned back her head for a kiss and got the fright of her life when she saw it was me instead of Otto.

'Cameron! You can't do that. He'll kill us both,' she said, pushing me away forcefully.

'Where is the humourless cretin anyway?'

'He's going over some recordings downstairs,' she said, looking distinctly nervous.

'Shame. No time for a quickie then,' I said, batting my lovely eyelashes.

She brushed me aside as she left the kitchen.

'*I* wouldn't bite you,' I whispered as she walked past me.

She stopped and as she turned to me, I could see tears welling up in her eyes. I took her in my arms and kissed her tenderly. *How dare he bite this princess!*

She pushed me away again looking scared.

'I do love him and if you care about me at all, you'd best leave well alone. He's under a lot of pressure. Nobody really trusts him, so he has to prove himself constantly. If there was any hint of him being anything other than an exceptional agent, they would get rid of him.'

'I'd never be their bitch!' I said without any sympathy for Otto's chosen situation. Then, flirting outrageously with her again I added, 'C'mon Stacey, let's run away together!'

At that point, the door opened and Otto came in. You didn't need to be a vampire to know that something had been going on between us. Calmly, he ordered Stacey downstairs and went about his business, as though nothing had happened, but it was the last time I saw Stacey.

Over the next few days, things were strained between Otto and me. The other agents felt it too and kept their heads down, getting on with their work largely in silence. Two vampires locking horns must have made for a pretty unpleasant working environment for them. Getting one of the agents, Chad, alone I enquired about Stacey and was told that Otto had put in an immediate transfer request for her. She was already back in Washington and due to start a new assignment the following week. I was relieved she was OK, but nobody dared mention her name in front of Otto again. They were all more than a little scared of the guy and there wasn't much friendly banter when he was in the room at the best of times. They followed his orders, but I could see that they found working for a vampire beyond weird. Otto was definitely not one of them and I wondered if he had any friends at all. I, at least, could leave in the evenings and spend time at Olga's.

***

One night, I decided to pick Olga up from work as she finished late enough in the evening for me to be able to go out. At eight o'clock, it was already dark so my hanging around outside the shop amongst the tourists attracted there by the fancy cars parked outside the Casino didn't draw attention. I made sure I stayed out of the way of camera lenses, though.

Suddenly, a girl wearing a black skirt, a blazer and trainers came whizzing by me. Her outfit was the uniform of any shop girl round here: a cheap synthetic suit that can be machine washed and doesn't require ironing and sensible footwear for running down the hill to catch the train. But a cold shiver went down my spine as I saw her darting nimbly around the tourists to avoid crashing into them as she hurried towards the station. *I know her!*

I couldn't resist following her and quickly caught up, staying just a few paces behind her. I texted Olga that I was sorry, but something had come up and I couldn't meet her. Then, remembering the tracker, I texted Otto with a message that I thought might keep me out of trouble:

Olga has other engagements. Taking the night off for some exercise and fresh local food. Heading by train to seaside village and promise not to cause problems. Cam X

We arrived on the platform and two minutes later the train to Cannes pulled in. I followed the girl on and managed to get a seat across from her. My phone beeped and I read Otto's response.

Get back here. Final warning!

I quickly replied:

Already on train. If I have to drink another bag of your rank blood, I'm gonna seriously barf! Not to worry, be back in a wee while ;)

Final warnings are never a good sign and the phone stayed eerily quiet after that. I tried to put Otto out of my mind and looked at the girl sitting across from me. Catching her eye, I asked, 'Are you Scottish?'

'How did you know?' she asked, astonished.

'Us pale faces tend to stand out a bit here in Monaco,' I said smiling warmly, but inside I had gone very cold. It was like sitting opposite a ghost, the pretty ghost of Fiona, my childhood sweetheart! The last time I had seen this face was when I left Edinburgh in 1915 and went off to war and there, sitting across from me, was a young woman who bore more than just a striking resemblance to her. The golden-brown hair was shorter than Fiona's had been and her clothes were somewhat different, but physically she was exactly the same; sparkling hazel eyes and that beautiful smile!

'What's your name?' I asked and her answer made my heart stop.

'Fiona,' she replied. 'Fiona Henderson.'

No way! Can this be her great granddaughter?

Gathering my wits, I reached across to shake her hand and said, 'Cameron Blair. Enchanté!'

As I recovered from the shock, we chatted enthusiastically about Scotland and our lives in France. I pretended to be a freelance photographer, hanging around Monaco hoping to get shots of celebrities. She worked in the same shop as Olga but I didn't let on that I knew her colleague. She was indeed from Edinburgh and had been living in France for nearly a year having moved there after university. A French friend from her course came from Cagnes-sur-Mer and her parents had offered Fiona their spare room to rent and to help her look for work.

'I thought why not? I did French in school and always wanted to improve it. It seemed a fun thing to do after university,' she told me.

'What did you study?' I asked.

'Law,' she said, rolling her eyes and it explained in an

223

instant why she was hanging around the Côte d'Azur rather than starting work in some stuffy lawyer's office.

'Family business?' I asked remembering Hootie's chosen profession.

'Aye, I come from a long line of barristers and lawyers,' she said with a big sigh.

She was now thinking of going back, however, as she'd decided the management at her work were a complete bunch of dicks. She didn't get on with the owner and one of the managers in the shop she described as 'an evil fucker'. Despite loving the warm climate and wanting to learn French she told me she couldn't stand it here much longer. She couldn't get used to the people and she missed Edinburgh and its laid back citizens.

'My arse of a boss flies off the handle over absolutely nothing,' she sighed. 'I have to keep telling myself he doesn't mean it and I shouldn't take it seriously, but it's hard not to get upset when somebody stands there shouting in your face.'

I was taken aback by her opening up to me so easily. I supposed she'd had a hard day and finding a fellow Scottish soul made her relax. I was amused by her rather colourful language, and by her narrative peppered liberally with the c- and f-words. I hadn't heard language like that since my last visit to Edinburgh and it gave me a warm feeling inside.

'How on earth did you ever manage to get a job in a high-end jewellers?' I asked smiling.

'What d'ye mean?' she said eyeing me with suspicion.

'I just hope you don't talk like that in front of the customers!'

'What? You're saying I'm too common!' she said, indignant, but I could see an amused twinkle in her eyes.

'I'm sure you come from an excellent background.

Finishing school in Lausanne perchance?' I mocked.

'I think I must sound a lot posher in French,' she giggled, then pulling her face into a grimace added, 'Plus I think they're hard-pushed to find workers, the way they treat their staff.'

'Don't sell yourself short lass. You have a lovely face and a smile that could liberate a credit card from the tightest owner's grasp.'

'Ah, thanks,' she responded, flashing that beautiful smile again.

Before I knew it, we were pulling into Cros de Cagnes station and she got up to leave. I got up too and followed her out when the train came to a halt.

'You live here too?' she asked, surprised at the coincidence, given that it was just a small seaside town.

'No, I don't, but the train has lost its charm now you're no longer on it.'

She burst out laughing. 'You're daft you are. So where do you live?'

'Monaco. Unless you fancy a drink, I'll return there on the next train.'

'You're in deep trouble now, pal. There are nae mair trains to Monaco tonight and the bars here shut at nine.'

She wasn't wrong. I was in deep trouble and I expected the CIA to pull up any minute and drag me off to subject me to some unpleasantness. I tried not to let it bother me, as I had found Fiona and was keen to get to know this reincarnation better.

'There's bound to be a hotel bar open somewhere. I'm expecting some friends to drag me off at any moment, but if they don't I could get a room and we could have a drink.'

'I'm not sure if I want to have a drink with a vampire.'

225

That drew me up short. *What the fuck?* Flabbergasted, I said, as coolly as I could, 'That's a strange thing to say. What makes you think–'

'No reflection in the train window,' she interrupted, 'and you're so pale, even by Scottish standards.' She looked me straight in the eye. She didn't seem afraid. She was more curious and maybe even a little excited.

I pondered for a moment, trying to think of a plausible way to explain the no-reflection thing, but she was so calm and direct that for some reason I trusted her. I decided just to be myself.

'Ok then…' I started, 'If you have a drink with me, I'll show you my fangs.'

I watched for her attitude to change, but she just looked quickly around her to check we weren't being observed and said, 'Ok then, show us!'

I sprang them as dramatically and scarily as I could, but it didn't faze her at all!

'Wow! That is *so* cool! I never thought I'd meet a real vampire!' she said and she put her hand up to my mouth to touch my fangs.

'If you play your cards right, you might even get to kiss one,' I said smiling cheekily now, as I withdrew my vampire teeth.

She giggled again, put her arm through mine and we headed towards the beach. I knew this place well as it was near to the racetrack, where I had come in better days to bet on the horses. There were a few small hotels on the seafront, but overall it was a quiet place with little nightlife.

'Are you gonnae kill me?' she asked, way too cheerfully for such question. I realised then that Fiona thought that maybe I was playing an elaborate trick on her. She'd seen some things she couldn't explain, thought I couldn't harm a fly and decided to play along to see what was really going on.

'No! I just want to get to know you.' I stopped her and looked into her eyes, trying to figure this girl out 'You don't really think I'm a vampire.'

'Mebbe ye are, mebbe ye arenae. But ye're a bloody good illusionist if ye arenae,' she jested in a thick Scottish accent. She pulled me towards the beach again; it was obvious she was enjoying this.

'So how many people have you killed? How old are you? What's it like to drink blood? Oh, and do you only kill virgins. Is that why you haven't pounced yet?'

While she fired a barrage of questions at me, she held on to my arm and laughed. *Bloody Hollywood. This is Roberto all over again.* I decided to humour her. Her eyes sparkled and she clearly wasn't easily shockable as Roberto had been.

'I was born in 1895 in Edinburgh and I became a vampire in 1915. Not sure how many folk I've killed but most people think it's too many and drinking blood is better than sex and any human will do!' I replied with a wink.

I was curious about her too. I had to know if there was a family connection. 'Did you have a great-grandmother called Fiona that was married to some dullard named Alistair Henderson?'

'Yes I did,' she said surprised, 'but I never knew her. She died in the 1960s I think. Why, did you know her?'

'We were engaged, but I never came back from the war so she was forced to marry that wet blanket Alistair,' I told her, feeling a little melancholy.

'Forced? Like, say, you got her up the duff?' asked Fiona shocked.

'No, no! I never got that far with her, but men must have

227

been scarce after the war for her to have married him!'

I realised I still hadn't quite got over the betrayal of my childhood friend Hootie who had snapped up my Fiona. New Fiona gave my arm a squeeze in sympathy. She seemed to find it quite sweet, this vampire that was still carrying a torch for her great granny.

'I can't believe you knew my great granny and then you just happened to be on the same train!' she exclaimed after some reflection. I had the impression she thought I was maybe pulling her leg with a far-fetched pickup line.

'I saw you on Casino Square and thought I'd seen a ghost. You're so like her. So I followed you to the train.'

We found a hotel bar open and Fiona said she could murder a pint of lager. I ordered two halves and told her she could drink mine too. We'd barely sat down when I saw a familiar car pull up. I quickly told Fiona not to get alarmed and that I had to go but that I would find her again. She was confused by my sudden departure and didn't manage to say anything before I dashed out of the door.

'Otto! So pleased you came to give me a lift. I just discovered that there are no more trains back to Monaco tonight,' I said airily, as I opened the car door and spotted Otto on the back seat.

'Get in,' he ordered.

'I was just in the process of ordering food. I can leave that, but I haven't got round to the other reason I came here for, a nice run along the beach front,' I protested and to my great surprise Otto told me I had half an hour. He must have learned from the French that I could be a lot of trouble if I didn't get to burn off some of my energy. I really wanted to continue my conversation with Fiona, but I went for a run instead to think about how I might get to see her again.

Chapter 25: Fiona

I had to see Fiona again and over the next few days I thought of little else. Olga noticed how distracted I was and thought I was just worried about my situation. She couldn't have been sweeter or more attentive and I almost felt sorry that I was using her to get to Andrei. Worse was to come, though. Now I was going to have to use her to get to Fiona too.

I was royally fed up with Otto and his crew. Chad, Steve and Bethany were so serious and they wouldn't have understood a good game of football if it had bitten them in the arse. Their stupid sports always took hours and hours and usually involved wusses in padded clothing chasing each other around a field with far too many lines on it. Otto and I didn't talk unless it was absolutely necessary and the operation to entrap Andrei was going nowhere. My days felt numbered. I needed to get away.

One night at Olga's I had an idea. I knew her place was bugged, but I didn't think there were any cameras – the CIA seemed oddly reluctant to watch as I invisibly did obviously unspeakable things to Olga for hours on end. After we got comfortable on the couch and started watching a film, I slipped her a note and gestured to her not to say a word. She looked at me, alarmed, but unfolded the note and read it.

Olga darling,
I think we are being bugged. Be very careful in what you say to me and on the telephone. Andrei is my friend and I think our enemies are getting closer. I do have someone here in Monaco that can help me, but I think I'm being followed so I can't contact her directly. Fiona, who works with you, can help me but she

doesn't know about me yet. Can you find out her work schedule and let me know, so I can contact her on the train? I know she lives in Cros de Cagnes. I am sorry that I will have to leave you again. I want you to know that I love you and that I'll find you again, but staying here now would result in my death.

It wasn't total fabrication and Olga bought it all. Her eyes teared up and she looked heartbroken. She'd clearly miss me dreadfully. Maybe I would send her a letter confessing to using her so she could move on with her life, but she'd still find it hard to find anyone to equal me.

She got me Fiona's work schedule for the next few weeks and the following night I wrote her a quick note asking her to suggest going for a walk, knowing that if Otto heard the idea coming from her he wouldn't think anything of it. We left the apartment and after checking the street around her, Olga asked, 'So who is Fiona really? She seems like an ordinary shop girl. She's always clowning around making us laugh by pulling faces behind the boss' back. How is she in a position to help you?'

'I've not met her,' I lied and then said, in my most mysterious voice, 'One of my contacts told me that she's a rogue British agent with a network that can help people disappear.'

'Wow! Her cover is really good then. She's always telling us stories about getting drunk and doing silly things, and it's all a lie.' Olga was impressed.

'Yep. So, she can get me a new identity and a safe address. Once I'm gone, you should tell Andrei to be on his guard and check for bugs, but wait until I'm gone,' I urged her. 'I don't want my enemies to know I'm on to them.'

'Yes, of course,' she agreed, but looked depressed again at

the prospect of my leaving.

We went back to her apartment and I gave her the extra special Cameron treatment – the kind that leads to waking up the neighbours and indeed that night to an alarmed knock on the door by Mrs Dumont asking if Olga was alright. When a flustered Olga opened the door wearing just a sheet and urged her not to call the police she realised what was going on fled back upstairs, blushing.

After that night, Olga saw very little of me and then only very late at night. Sometimes I woke her at three o'clock in the morning and she never told me to get lost, even though it was clear she'd been sound asleep and was very tired.

***

I made a complete nuisance of myself meanwhile, saying I was going to Olga's and then running off to take a train to a seaside town, picking a different one each time. They always got there a wee while later with their car to give me a lift back, and I hoped they'd grow tired of it and leave me be eventually. But they were a dogged lot. Otto was not impressed and along with long, tedious lectures became quite inventive with his punishments. I don't like having my kneecaps smashed with a baseball bat or being shot at and the severing of my little finger was particularly unpleasant – *it won't grow back!* – but these things had to be endured if I wanted to get away once and for all and survive.

About three weeks in, Otto decided he really couldn't be bothered any more and I noticed that the boys began to take longer to retrieve me each time. I think it was as a result of the wee script I had written for Olga to read out to me about something Tatiana had supposedly told her. It read: 'Darling,

Tatiana mentioned today that she'd overheard Andrei talking to someone on his mobile and saying something about "missile" and "delivery" and a south sea orchid. She thought that might be a ship's name...'

That'd send them on a wild goose chase, trying to find a fictional ship! Even better, it turned out that the *South Sea Orchid* did exist. It was an Australian fishing boat and the CIA had the Australian secret service monitor it for a few days just in case. I think it probably strained Australian-American relations when the Australians boarded the boat and found nothing more illegal than five grams of hashish. Otto studied my reaction intently as he told me the saga, but I'm very good at playing the innocent and not even my big brother managed to sniff me out.

So eventually, when things were feeling less intense, I decided to get on the same train as Fiona again one night. She seemed pleased to see me.

'I'm glad you're ok,' she said as we took a seat on the 20.43 train. 'That was disturbing, your "friends" taking you away like that. I've done a lot of thinking since our last meeting and I'm starting to think you're the real deal'

'I am!'

'So what's going on with these "friends" of yours?'

'Some people believe that my kind shouldn't be allowed to roam free,' I said resigned

'That's terrible! Next thing you know they'll rip out yer fangs,' she said sarcastically.

'Don't give them any ideas. Anyway, they can take my fangs, but they will *never* take my freedom,' I defiantly quoted *Braveheart*. She giggled but told me it was just a bit too cheesy.

'I need to get out of here, Fiona!' I sighed.

'Me and all, Cameron. Christ if I have to endure another

hour-long rant by my bampot boss about the aircon I'm gonnae scream! I mean, there he was complaining again that he'd get a cold if we lowered the heating from 26 to 25 degrees. Meanwhile I'm dressed in my skimpy summer dress and still sweating like a pig!'

I had to interrupt her there to tell her off. 'A lady doesn't sweat, Fiona. She perspires,' I admonished.

I got a punch on the arm for my sarcasm before she continued, 'So I'm standing there *perspiring* like a pig while it is fucking minus ten outside.'

'Minus ten!' I cried. 'In Monaco? In spring? I must have missed that. Did it snow too?'

I received another punch on the arm, but she hit like a girl and it was cute rather than painful. Truth was, I felt very comfortable with her and could have listened to her all day.

'Ye ken what I mean,' she said laughing.

'Aye – that the man is a dick!'

'No. That the man is a total and utter dick!'

Then she got serious and asked me if I was in trouble and I told her everything – about Otto and his mission and about my relationship with Olga. I was curious as to whose side she would take on that one. We got to her station too soon and she got up to leave.

'Don't tell Olga anything,' I urged her. 'I will tell her myself eventually.'

'Ok,' she said and picked up her bag.

'I'll see you soon,' I said and remained seated.

She gave me a questioning look, but then she was gone. I stayed on the train till Cannes and had a walk around the marina. It was a bad mistake – my boat was still moored there. The police must have auctioned it off and the new owner had re-christened her the *Daisy Mae*. *You've got to be shitting me!*

Daisy Mae? Recognising my yacht depressed me, so when the agents caught up with me I wasn't my usual cheery, mischievous self and they were rightly cautious. They handcuffed me and had some silverwear at the ready, to combat any resistance. After a bag of O positive I went to my room and didn't speak to anyone all the next day.

Risky as it was, I decided to go and see Fiona again the next night.

'If I asked you, would you help me?' I said as soon as we sat down on the train.

'Me? Why would I help you? By your own admission you do some pretty horrible things. Maybe Otto is right to take you off the streets,' she said searching my face as though trying to find the evil written on my baby face.

'I haven't killed anyone for ages. Most of the time I'm rather charming,' I said, batting my eyelashes.

'Fuck off! I bet you want to bite me right now!' she said, pushing me away playfully.

'You do look tasty,' I said trying to kiss her neck, but her hand pushed me away – harder this time.

I got serious and asked her again if she'd help. She said she needed to think about it, so we talked about work and Fiona told me a lot about Olga and how the manager always picked on someone during the day. Thinking he was funny, he'd make prank phone calls, but he could be nastier and often blamed Olga or Fiona for mistakes he'd made.

'The bastard hit her with a safe-door today,' she told me furiously.

'What? He can't get away with that!' I exclaimed, anger welling up.

'Olga said it was an accident, but I think the prick did it deliberately.'

'Why doesn't she tell him to fuck off and leave her be?' I asked, disturbed at this news.

'You know Olga. She has such a kind heart and always sees the best in people. I don't know how good your French is, but mine and Olga's isn't perfect which makes it harder to fight back. I went to the bosses once and told them about this guy's behaviour, as best I could in French. But then he just gets to go and explain his version of the story much more eloquently so they always take his side!'

Fiona went on to tell me she'd often find Olga in tears at lunchtime. I'd had no idea she had such a miserable time at work. She'd never bothered me with her troubles. I decided I would kill this man as a going away present to Olga.

'Are you thinking of killing this guy?' asked Fiona suddenly, horrified when I didn't say anything for a while. My smug smile at the thought of taking him out must have been too obvious.

'Wow, you read my mind. Would you be upset if I did? Sounds like your workplace would improve without him,' I asked light-heartedly.

'You can't just go about killing people because they're arses.'

'I've killed people for less. Be honest, would you be upset?' I asked more seriously.

'No. I've wished him dead many times,' and with those words Fiona revealed her darker side. She blushed and turned away as soon as she had said it.

She was definitely not her great grandmother; that Fiona would never have wished anybody dead or even sworn for that matter. I didn't mind, I actually liked the darker, rougher Fiona a lot and it was almost like my Fiona had changed in line with me over the years. I realised then that I didn't just want her to help me, I wanted her to come with me and share her life with me. Before I could say anything else the train pulled into her station.

'Don't do it,' she said suddenly as she got ready to leave. 'I don't want a dead man on my conscience.' And then she kissed my cheek fleetingly and nearly ran off the train. I could tell she didn't really mean those last words though. It would be on my conscience alone and killing an arse that was making two lovely lassies miserable was enough to quiet mine.

***

Two nights later, Fiona's manager was found dead in his car. The police launched an investigation into what was a rather puzzling crime. They could see only the manager on the parking garage CCTV and nothing else to explain his weird death. I had followed him from the shop into the underground car park and when he'd unlocked and opened his car door I'd pounced. All the police could see on the footage was the man grabbing his neck as he fell into his car. They saw his legs kick for a while before he just dangled, lifeless, from his car seat. I'd disguised my fang marks by planting some glass shards into his neck. Figuring out where the shards had come from and what had propelled them with such deadly force into this man's neck would surely have them baffled for years!

The night after, I found Olga at home in tears. She was wracked with guilt as she had wished an accident on this man and then one had happened. She was inconsolable. I didn't understand her; it wasn't like she'd had anything to do with the accident or even liked the guy. I decided that Olga was too nice for her own good. She deserved better, but was probably never going to get it. Fiona on the other hand took the news differently.

'You fucking did it, didn't you!' she hissed as soon as she spotted me on the platform two nights later. Her eyes looked feverish and I could hear her heart pounding. She was certainly stressed, but she wasn't upset.

'I don't know what you're talking about,' I said in mock innocence.

'Man! He got some glass rammed into his neck. You're fucking brutal!'

'Who? And why would I be involved?' I asked, feigning indignation.

The train pulled in at that point and I followed Fiona on board and took the seat beside her. She looked out of the window for a while, pretending I wasn't there and playing nervously with her handbag until she broke the zip with her fidgeting.

'Now look what you made me do,' she said angrily, showing me the broken off toggle.

'How?'

'You come into my life turning everything upside down!'

'I still don't see how that broke the zip on your handbag,' I replied, really getting confused now.

'Fuck it! I will help you,' she said turning to face me, and her eyes were wild and glazed as though she was drunk, but I smelled no alcohol in her blood. She was intoxicated by the feeling of having had a hand in killing someone, drunk on the power that, if she said the word, I could make something bad happen. In spite of herself, Fiona was excited.

'Come with me, Fiona,' I blurted out. 'I can't promise it'll be all easy, but I'll give you the experience of a lifetime.'

She looked at me, flushed, and stammered, 'What about Olga?'

'Do you see Olga as Bonnie to my Clyde?' I asked drily.

'She's daft about you,' said Fiona, turning away from me again. Her heart was pounding even harder.

'She'll get over me and, let's face it, she's better off without me,' I murmured. I was glad she was turned away as for a brief moment I felt sorry for what I had done to Olga and questioned my decision to involve Fiona. Asking her to accompany a vampire on the run could be dangerous. I was again engaging innocent humans for my own needs.

We sat in silence for a while, but the train was moving ever closer to its destination so I shook off my reservations and started to explain my plan to Fiona. It entailed my being totally reliant on her, so she would have to decide now if she really wanted to do this and I would have to put complete trust in her if she did. She listened to me silently and then she dug out her diary and made a few notes.

'OK. We'll do it next Friday. I think I can have everything in place by then. I'll be on the 20.13 train.'

'And will you come with me?'

'Dunno,' and with that she got up and left. I watched her walking along the platform, grim-faced and deep in thought.

I got off in Biot and jogged along the deserted seafront. When the agents caught up with me I was even more chipper than usual. On our return, I informed Otto that I'd had some more ideas and told him it would be best now to set up a meeting with Andrei. There was an exhibition opening at a gallery in Cannes the following Friday and I would make sure, through Olga, that Andrei would be there. I said I'd go there by train, so the agents would have time to set everything up before I arrived. Otto didn't agree to this. He was mightily suspicious of my recent fascination with trains.

I pulled out a wee booklet. 'OK, you got me. I didn't want to admit it, but I've taken up a new hobby, and I'm not particularly proud of it.' I showed Otto the pages of neatly jotted down train numbers, dates and times.

'I was wondering why your computer history contained mostly French train sites. I've been wracking my brain for days over what you were searching for.' He looked at me as if I was quite deranged. 'I'm beginning to wonder if there is any truth in the idea that vampires can go senile.'

'We need to keep our minds occupied, Otto. Dad had his chess, I'm into trains and you... I suppose, you have your work, though you must be getting pretty bored of that by now.' I rolled my eyes. 'I mean, all this spy shit must get a bit tedious. All you seem to do is listen into conversations and watch hours of CCTV footage.'

I was sure Otto was convinced that I was really quite thick and foolish. Erratic behaviour fitted my profile perfectly. I don't think he had any idea that I was tunnelling out from beneath him.

'Still, you're not taking the train. You and I will follow along in my car.'

'As you wish, but there is a rumour that they're putting a new Bombardier locomotive on the 20.13 slot.'

'Tough!'

That was the end of the conversation, but I didn't mind. The revised plan left me plenty to work with.

Chapter 26: Champagne

I was a bundle of nerves for the rest of that week, but I tried to behave as if nothing was up. I knew Otto wasn't stupid and would suss me out if I showed my nerves. I was at least certain that nobody knew anything about Fiona and that all my preparations were being carried out by her. I co-operated seriously with the agents to set up the meeting with Andrei. Surveillance equipment would be everywhere in the gallery to record our meeting, or his side of it at least. The owner was made aware and he agreed to let the CIA set up shop on the premises. It was a stroke of luck that he was American and patriotic. Olga was aware only that I wanted to meet Andrei and she called Tatiana to arrange a meeting at the gallery that Friday, saying she wanted them both to meet her new boyfriend who was an art dealer. It turned out that Andrei had intended to go to the opening anyway, so all was going according to plan.

Then Friday came and all the agents descended on Cannes leaving me and Otto alone to wait for nightfall. Otto was busy tweaking the sound and pictures on the recording equipment, so busy that he didn't notice me coming up behind him with a very sharp stake. I had spent the whole week sharpening the end of a broom handle I'd taken from Olga's apartment. Now my arm reached over his shoulder and I rammed the stake into his chest as hard as I could. His body crumbled instantly, leaving just his suit, his watch and a little cone of dust. I looked at the sorry pile, but felt nothing; we might have been the same vampire bloodline, but that hadn't made us friends. We'd wanted different things and had agreed on very little.

One thing we had coincided on, however, now lay amongst

the dust on the floor and I smiled smugly as I picked up the Breguet, put it on my own wrist and shoved Otto's wallet into my pocket. Then I made my way to the train station and waited for Fiona. She came belting up the escalator seconds before the train arrived.

'Oh my god! I ran flat out to get here, we were absolutely heaving today,' she puffed, her face bright red. 'I should've told them to shove their job up their arses seeing as it was my last day, but despite what you might think, I'm too polite.'

I was too nervous to make a joke or sympathise fully. I just asked anxiously, 'Is everything ready?'

'Aye,' she said and as we boarded the train she gave my hand a reassuring squeeze.

We went straight into the loo together, which drew some disgusted looks from our fellow passengers. Fiona opened up her bag and pulled out a scalpel, tweezers and some gauze.

'I've never cut anyone, I'm not sure if I can do it,' she said looking apprehensive.

'I'm not human. I promise I'll heal as soon as you cut me. Don't worry,' I assured her. I took the hand holding the scalpel and cut into my own arm to let her see how quickly I healed.

'Ok then,' she said with more confidence.

I turned round in the small space and she felt my neck for the small tracker. She took some deep breaths and then cut into my skin like a skilful surgeon, quickly pulling the tracker out with the tweezers and stemming the flow of blood with some gauze. She told me to press down for a few seconds and then cleaned everything up with some wet wipes. 'That's amazing! The wound has already healed up and there's not even a scar,' she said stroking my neck.

'Well done you,' I said, turning around in the small toilet

and having a good look at the device she handed me.

We decided to let the tracker ride on to its final destination: Grasse. My mobile travelled along with it in the bathroom bin. Getting off at Cros de Cagnes, we walked to where Fiona had parked the hire car. The back seat was laden with large bags. I picked the girl up and spun her around planting a big kiss on her lips.

'It better be worth it, Mr Blair. I've never done anything this stupid and reckless in all my life,' she said struggling to get loose.

'It won't be boring, I promise you that,' I said squeezing her tightly.

I put her down and we drove off towards Marseille airport where she had agreed to hand the car back. On the way, she told me she had resigned from work earlier in the week and made everyone believe she was going home to Scotland. No one would think anything of her absence. Only Olga would know our mutual disappearance was related and no doubt she would just cry and pray for our safety. I looked at Fiona and wondered again if I was being totally selfish or whether I really believed I could enrich this girl's life. She gave me a big grin and her eyes lit up with anticipation. She'd run off with a big bad vampire and she was loving every second of it.

'I did kill your manager,' I said, suddenly serious. 'You can change your mind any time you want.'

'I know, but to be fair he was an evil scumbag,' she said mercilessly. She grinned and turned towards me. 'I just want to know everything about you. You're a fucking vampire! How cool is that?'

I felt I needed to tell her a few more facts about myself. I had to be fair to the girl. If she didn't like what she heard now, she would be able to take a flight home to Edinburgh and forget all about me. If I was getting involved with someone again, it had to be the truth and nothing but the whole nasty truth.

'Look Fiona. I won't bite you, but I will have to bite other people. Some nights I will go out to a nightclub, pick someone up and go back to her place. I will sleep with her if I feel like it and then drug her and drink some of her blood.'

'Ok...' she said hesitantly. 'I'm not your girlfriend, so do what you want, but why wouldn't you want to bite me?'

'I can't see you as food. I don't think it's healthy to feed on people you have a relationship with. I believe that would be submissive from your part, and what I like about you is that you're anything but!'

'Oh!'

I needed to frighten her a bit more, test her.

'I do also feed on dogs. I steal, I'm greedy and vindictive and if I see you with another man, I'll probably kill him in a fit of jealous rage.'

'Yeah, but apart from murdering, stealing, drugging women and eating dogs, you're really kind and cuddly,' she said with a smile.

'I like to think so!' I relented. I had opened my black heart to her and she hadn't jumped out of the car. If anything, her cheeks had become more flushed and her heart was beating faster with excitement. I took my hand off the wheel and squeezed hers. There was one final thing to say that might discourage her.

'And lastly, don't think for a minute you can change me. If anything, I get more evil as time goes by.'

'I'll think I'll write a book about you, Cameron! You're over a hundred years old so you must have some stories to tell. I'll publish a best-seller and become a millionaire!' She threw her arms up in imagined triumph.

I certainly did have some good stories to tell and loved telling them! Maybe this alliance was a good idea and Fiona would get exactly the experience she wanted.

'Just promise me you'll let me go if I ever want to leave,' she suddenly said, quietly.

'I promise,' I said solemnly, but right then I desperately wanted her to stay with me. I wanted to show her the world and give her everything it had to offer, by legal or illegal means.

We arrived at the airport car hire a few hours later and then it was up to me. I had to go off and steal a car while Fiona took a shuttle bus into town with all her bags. People would see her on CCTV but not me and while a car driving itself out of a car park might raise eyebrows if it was spotted, Fiona would not be implicated. I found a nice German motor and drove into town to pick Fiona up near the main St Charles station. We both let out a long sigh of relief as we drove away.

'So what now?' she said.

'It's your adventure. Where do you want to go?' I asked.

'Where do they make champagne? I could do with a drink.'

She could not have said anything better! 'Oh, I'm so glad I found you again Fiona! You really are a woman after my own heart. Champagne it is!' And I steered the car towards the motorway.

For more information about Angela Lockwood, Cameron Blair and the Language in the Blood series, visit:

http://www.cruftslover.adzl.com/

https://www.facebook.com/CruftsloverAkaCameronBlair

Other books by this author available on Amazon:

Something Short

by Elspeth Morrison and Angela Lockwood

Something Short is a collection of short stories from French and Scottish shores by two female writers; Elspeth Morrison and Angela Lockwood. We meet a variety of interesting and amusing Scottish characters in Begonia, The Wee Baldy Man, The Pop Star and a mad scientist in Animals, but also some personal experiences in dealing with arthritis and depression in Begonia and The Goldfish Bowl. The stories are short but impactful and we hope they leave a lasting impression on you.

You're not alone

An Indie Author Anthology

By Ian D. Moore and Friends (Angela Lockwood, contributor)

An international group of indie authors, inspired by the personal grief of one, decided to collaborate in the spring of 2015 in a project to create this multi-genre smorgasbord of original short stories, all with the same potent theme – relationships. Some are heartfelt, some funny, some poignant, and some are just a little bit scary – much like relationships themselves. All are by authors fired by the shared enthusiasm to give something back in aid of Macmillan Cancer Support. Cancer touches us all. It has in some way affected those who have contributed their time and talent here. This is our way of showing that we care.

Indie authors carry forward a revolutionary shift in publishing, which allows the author to be creative director in their own work. There are many exceptional, experienced and acclaimed writers who have decided to take this bold step in publishing. In producing this anthology we have also had the inestimable assistance on board of artists, graphic designers, and bloggers – all of whom have a place in our acknowledgments. You, the discerning reader, are the other vital part of this equation. By buying this book you are supporting the work of indie authors, as well as discovering their worth. You are also supporting the charity to which we have chosen to dedicate our work.

100% of the royalties earned or accrued in the purchase of this book, in all formats, will go to the Pamela Winton tribute fund, which is in aid of Macmillan Cancer Support.

www.ingramcontent.com/pod-product-compliance
Lightning Source LLC
Chambersburg PA
CBHW071955040426
42447CB00009B/1336

Acts of the Apostles

in Ten Minutes a Day

Mason Barge

ISBN: 979-8-9929596-0-4

TABLE OF CONTENTS

Acts in Ten Minutes a Day

Acts in Ten Minutes a Day

Acts in Ten Minutes a Day

Day 35 - Philip and the Ethiopian Eunuch (2) ... 67